Understanding Women:
The Definitive Guide to Meeting, Dating and Dumping, if Necessary

Understanding Women:
The Definitive Guide to Meeting, Dating and Dumping, if Necessary

By

Romy Miller

The Book Factory

Understanding Women:
The Definitive Guide to Meeting, Dating and Dumping, if
Necessary
by
Romy Miller

The Book Factory
an imprint of New Tradition Books
ISBN 1932420207

For RKR

Contents

My mission: To turn you into a dating machine.

Let's face facts. You probably don't know anything about women. Don't be upset. You know it's true. You need help, don't you? This isn't going to be easy but it's time, isn't it? Yeah, you know it is.

You've tried to meet someone but haven't had a date in a long time. You can't even remember the last time you *spoke* with a woman. In fact, the last woman you saw naked was on the internet.

I feel your pain, buddy, I really, really do.

And you've done everything in your power to hook up—from internet dating services to dating books. None of it helped. Mostly because you rarely get what you see on a computer—from a sweater to a woman it never looks quite the same. And those books were mostly written by men. Most men don't really have a clue as to what women really want or even what they're all about. That's because men's perception of women is an entirely different thing than how women actually are. They're just as confused as you are! Some might have a smidgen of good advice but if I wanted advice about women, I would go to the source—a woman.

It's not your fault that you're just an average Joe. You have an average job and lead an average life. Or maybe you're one of those internet millionaires and still can't seem to get a date. Regardless of your social status, there's help for you unless you have a tail and horns. Or webbed feet. (If you do, my apologies.)

Perhaps you've had a lot of dates but nothing seems to come out of them. You might be to the point where you've given up on it all. You've thrown in the towel and told yourself that women, simply, aren't worth it. You've been rejected and scorned and hey, maybe someone *threw* something at you. But you're not a bad guy, are you? No. You just can't figure chicks out. What do they want? Why do they behave in the manner they do? Why are they so elusive? And why do I still want them when they don't seem to want me?

I'm gonna help you with all that.

Let's talk about why you feel the way you do. I mean, not the rejected part, but the part that still wants women. Simply put, you have a biological imperative to mate. It's ingrained in you to go after a chick that you find attractive, mate with her and have a baby. *Whoa!*—you say—*nobody said anything about babies!* Listen, Einstein, that's why you want it. Sure, it's fun but the bottom line is you want to get your rocks off and the reason you want to is because you want to spread your genes. Getting a baby may not be what you want, but it's definitely what your hormones are screaming for. It's called "biology".

I told you this wasn't going to be easy.

That's why these feelings never go away and torture you on an every day—if not every hour—basis. You can't run away from it, you will never escape it. You need women like women need new shoes.

Heavy, huh? No, it doesn't have to be.

So, if it's all "biological", why are chicks so hard to figure out? Since the advent of the Independent Woman, it seems as though men have been left by the way-side. Women don't have to be as interested as they used to be. She can hire a handy-man to fix that leaky faucet and she can go to a sperm bank for a baby and she can buy a vibrator to please herself. So why does she need to expend the effort to meet you?

Again, it's all biological.

She does want you. She does need you. She's just gotten a little pickier and a little more ornery over the past few decades. However, we, as humans, are wired to want each other and not battery operated devices that give mind-blowing, though albeit, short orgasms. We have to have each other. We crave each other. We are horny for each other. Without each other...well, why bother with any of it?

That's where I come in.

So why did *I* write a book like this anyway? What makes *me* such an expert on this tantalizing subject? After all, I could make a lot more money doing internet porn. Well, think about it. Men don't understand women. I don't care how many degrees they have, they don't get it. I am a woman. That's all the creditability I need. I've also dated a few men in my time and you can learn from *their* mistakes.

Be warned, I am taking the cruel to be kind approach. Sometimes you will think I am a bitch from hell. I don't care. I am going to straighten you out. Someone has to or you're never going to get laid or ever have the opportunity for a woman to make your life miserable. I am going to tell you how women tick. What makes them tick. And why they tick. I will dispel the rumors, the half-truths. I will turn you into a dating machine and you will have your pick of any beautiful woman you want. You'll wonder why you didn't try this sooner.

Not only that, I'm going to tell you what to do *after* you get that date. I am going to tell you how to keep her—that is, if you want to keep her—after it's all said and done and some practical advice on sex. With this information at your disposal, it won't take long to get what you want and deserve.

Most chapters are going to be short and sweet, just like me. Mostly because it shouldn't take a gazillion years to explain something as simple as women and their womanly wiles. As you read this stuff, you might say to yourself, *"A lot of this is just common sense."* Apparently, no, it isn't. If it's common sense, why are so many of you out there making jerks out of yourselves?

If you follow my advice in this book, you will what is commonly known as a "Catch". Even if your relationships have never worked out before, take some of my advice, if not all, and the word will get around about you and how great you are. Hopefully, after you read this, you are going to be so cool that women are going to be asking *you* out. Know how to treat her right and the rest will follow. The more you know, the better you can understand the dynamics of that wonderful creature we call *Woman.*

So let's get started. We've got a lot of work to do.

The basic rules of dating women.

You will notice that there appears to be a lot of double standards in the dating world. Like, why are guys always expected to pay for dinner? (I still don't understand why men get so hung up on this.) Yes, there are a lot of double standards but so what? You wanna get lucky or not? If so, learn that just because something's a double standard doesn't mean you can change it for all mankind by simply refusing to give into it. You need to know that there are plenty of smart men out there who don't let little things like this get in the way of dating and/or getting lucky. They know there's a price to pay and they're more than willing to shell out. If you're not willing, then internet porn was created for a reason, wasn't it?

I have a feeling that some of you may think that you don't have to work for it. That you should be able to date a woman simply based on the merit that you have a penis. You can't. One reason is because there are gazillion penises out there. What makes yours so special? You have to work for it. You have to let a woman know you're worth it. You may have a million excuses but when you look at them close enough, maybe they all add up to the fact that you're afraid you'll expend the effort and get nothing in return. Will this happen? Who knows? But know that if you never try, you can never hope to hook up.

Some excuses:
- I don't have any money.
- I don't have enough confidence.
- Women don't like me.
- I don't have the looks.

These are just excuses for you not to get up off your butt and do something. That's all. If you're looking for an excuse, you *will* find it. Ask yourself if you really and truly want to spend the rest of your life alone. If you do, fine. Say hello to your comic book collection for me. If not, let's get to work.

But before we go any further, I am going to concentrate this chapter on the basics of women and of dating. This isn't every single thing included in the book. It's just a basic overview that should give you a general idea of what's going on.

The basic rules of women:
- Each and every one of them is unique. Once you figure one of them out, another will throw you a curve ball. There's nothing you can do about it, either.
- Not all women are unapproachable and that includes very beautiful women. Sometimes, very beautiful women aren't approached *because* of their beauty. Many men are afraid of rejection and don't approach them. So they appreciate what little attention they get. (As long as you're not a dork.)
- Women love to talk and they especially love to talk about themselves. If you can get her to talk about herself, all you have to do is nod occasionally and pay attention to what she's

saying. (Or, at the very least, pretend to pay attention.)

- No woman likes to be perceived as easy, even if she is.
- Women love gifts.
- Women are picky about everything. Why wouldn't she be picky about who she dates? You have to make it worth her time.
- Women like to date men who are worth it to her. If you're a "fixer-upper" with bad clothes, body and teeth, she's not going to expend the effort. Unless, of course, you've just won the lottery.
- Women love to be seduced, romanced and pampered.
- Women are in control. This is the biggest thing you will ever learn. In dating, women are totally in control. You, obviously, plan the date, but she calls the shots and it's her decision if you have sex or not.
- On the flip side of this, women want a man who takes control in the bedroom. If you can rock her world, you'll never get rid of her.

The basic rules of dating:

- While you do not have to be extraordinary good looking or rich you do need to be: Clean, in good, physical shape, sharply dressed and smell nice.
- Do anything and everything you can do to improve yourself. That includes getting a better paying job, driving a manly car, and having a nice, clean apartment or house.
- Never brag or lie. It's always best to present an honest image. If you start to date a woman, she's going to find out about you eventually anyway.

- There are three types of men: the Confident Man, the Bad Boy and the Smart Guy. Learn to combine elements from all three of these types and you should have women falling all over you.
- Never allow a woman to pay for anything, even if she insists.
- Clothes do matter.
- Good grooming matters, too.
- Never invite yourself over to a chick's apartment. She will assume *you* assume she's a slut. No woman wants to be perceived as easy—see basic rules of women.
- It is up to you to date. If you don't take the initiative, then nothing will ever happen. Women will not come to you. You have to go to them.
- Never insult a woman.
- Never try to get a woman in bed.
- Never hit a woman.
- Never disrespect a woman even if she does it to you. Just take it like a man and she'll be the one who looks bad.
- Never think that you deserve to get laid just because you paid for dinner.
- The main thing you need is confidence. Confidence to dress nice. Confidence to approach women. Confidence to get rejected without it killing you. Confidence, confidence, confidence!

Ready, set, go!

I know you're ready to hit the streets and turn yourself into a dating machine, but first things first. You need to mentally prepare yourself for your new adventures in dating. And by this I mean, get yourself physically and mentally ready.

Let me say one more thing. I know there are a lot of whiners out there who will whimper when they realize they're not perfect. They'll also cry when they realize that they are going to have to improve on themselves so they can get date. Improving yourself by buying new clothes or getting rid of your beer belly doesn't have to kill you. In fact, it's only going to help you.

An important thing to keep in mind is that not *every* chick you run across is going to dig you. There are some chicks out there who really don't like anyone for whatever reason. That's life. All you have to do is weed those chicks out. Don't beat yourself up if you get rejected a few times. Expect it and then when you finally get some acceptance, it will be all the sweeter.

Always remember that while this may be a lot to consume, it is the winners who do stuff that losers don't want to do. Winners will take chances and search for opportunity. If you're not willing to get up off the couch and improve on yourself, you haven't got a chance in hell in scoring.

One of the most important things to do before you try to pick up a girl is to go out and observe them. Sounds stupid, but be a girl watcher. Watch how she acts and what she does. Watch couples together. Watch other guys trying to pick up chicks. Learn from their mistakes. Watch, listen, observe. Take time to do this. It's important to know what you're up against. (Also, don't be too obvious when you do this. You don't want to give the "voyeur" vibe off.)

What we learned:
- You have to improve on yourself.
- Not all women are going to dig you, just like you don't dig all women.
- Don't be afraid of rejection. I know it can hurt, but if you never try, you never give anyone an opportunity to say yes.

But I just want to get laid!

Maybe all you want is some poontang. You lament, *All I want to do is get laid. Tell me how to get laid for God's sake! I don't care about all this other stuff!* It's all about the sex to you, isn't it? If so, go hire a hooker. It's really pretty simple, if that's all you want.

Do you really want to be one of those guys who use women just for sex? Let me tell you, the word will get out pretty quickly on your bad habits. Girls talk, guys, and if the word gets out, you're going to be in even worse condition than when you started. Also, by doing this, you put yourself at risk for all kinds of diseases. Any skank will have sex with you if you get her drunk enough. But if you want a good/real woman who doesn't necessarily have to get liquored up to have sex with you, you are going to have to put in some effort. Like it or lump it. If you want to find someone and, as Desmond Morris says, form a pair bond, then you are going to have to work a little.

Of course you're saying, *but I don't care about the pair bond* and if you are, shame on you! You just need to sit, back, relax and open your eyes. By the time I am finished with you, getting laid will be the least of your worries. If you're still not convinced, go on. Put the book down and try it *your* way. Let me know how it works out.

Let me outline a few facts for you. Getting laid is great and it feels wonderful. Believe me, I know. But if all you ever do is hop from one bed to another and never form any sort of relationship, you're going to end up alone. Think about your uncle. The one who's alone and drinks a lot. The one who smells funny and tells dirty jokes no one gets. Is this what you want? Do you want to end up like your uncle? No, you don't. And you don't have to! However, if you don't work on this stuff—yourself mainly—then it won't matter how many women you have sex with, you always feel alienated from them. Besides, how can you expect to have sex with women if you don't understand how they operate?

Women are your friends; they're your buddies. You've just got to learn about them and learn how to work them. There are no real dating techniques. What works for one won't work for another. There are some universal truths, however, and that's what we're going to concentrate on. Once you're ready to face up to the truth, then and only then can you be ready to go out and pursue the woman of your dreams, whoever she may be. Once you know what you're dealing with, you can approach any woman out there with confidence. And if you get her in bed and then want to leave her, that's your business. All I can say is if that's what you're after, then you've got some real intimacy issues to work on. And that's your problem.

Chances are if you're reading this book, you're lonely and don't have that someone special in your life. Am I right? You want to take that step in the right direction and get your life moving. You do want a family on down the line but nothing seems to be working right now. No matter how hard you try, something isn't clicking.

Or, are you trying too hard? Maybe. Maybe you're not really trying at all. But I can tell you this, the more effort you put into getting dates and forming pair bonds, the more you will get out. If you do this, you will have a person you can share stuff with. You will always have a date on Saturday nights. And isn't that much better than going to Ladies' Night?

I think so.

You also need to realize that women are just as confused about men as you are them. For the most part, none of us have you figured out. We want to know what makes you tick as much as you want to know what makes us tick. We're all so fascinated with each other. But that doesn't keep us from playing mind games does it?

Nope. And then it all gets tangled and messy and weird. How can we hook up with each other with as little pain as possible? How the hell can a man approach a woman without worrying about getting his head bitten off?

I think one of the main problems in the dating world is that we tend to over-intellectualize everything. We overanalyze and try to second guess everyone's next move. We don't give people enough time to react or, for that matter, to size us up before we're all over them, trying to impress them. Then we're kicking ourselves for even talking to them. Hooking up should not be as hard as it is, but for some reason, it's hard as hell.

Because we over-intellectualize everything, everything gets skewed and that makes everyone a bit crazy. That's why it's so hard to walk up to a chick and ask her out on a date. What if she says no? How about this? *What if she says yes?*

After I'm done with you, she might.

Don't believe me? Then that tells me you are one of the walking wounded. Do not be one of the walking wounded. If you think that chicks will reject you before you even ask them out, they probably will. It's all in your attitude. If you look and feel good about yourself, then other people will see that too. You can't feel sorry for yourself anymore. It hasn't worked in the past, has it? You need to learn to shrug off rejection. It will smart for a while but the more comfortable you become with yourself, the better off you will be. And the easier everything will get.

Know this: There is no instant gratification. Unless you're a rock star, you are not going to get laid easily. Stop running away. Stop asking for an easier way. There is no easy way to date. None! You will have to work to get what you want. It's up to you. No one can help you but you. I want this book to be a wake-up call for you men who have failed at relationships or who have never even gotten one off the ground. And if all you do want to do is get laid, how about this? How about getting laid with someone who cares about you? Who will enjoy being around you? That's much better than picking up the random ho to party with. Once you find someone special, your life will be special. You will have stuff to look forward to. Places to go. New people to meet and new experiences to have. And it all starts here. Right here. Right now. Today. It starts with you.

I can hear you saying, "Yeah, I'll do this tomorrow." Fine. And tomorrow, you can put it off again. Why not start it today? Right now? This instant. Own up to whatever it is in your past that has gotten you down. Face it like a man and then move on from it. Heal yourself. You don't have to do drugs or go to a psychologist to figure out what's wrong with you. Look inside yourself—and not in a new-agey kinda way—and figure out what's blocking you from living the life you want to. Face your fears of isolation or being unsuccessful or whatever they may be. Once you do that, everything will fall into place.

The old cliché says, "Never put off tomorrow what you can do today." And why should you put it off? There's no real reason. The sooner you get it done, the sooner you can find your beautiful girl.

Okay. Stop rolling your eyes. I'll stop with the psychobabble for now. We have many important things to discuss.

What we learned:

- If getting laid is all you're after, there are plenty of women out there who get paid for such things.
- We all need someone special in our lives.
- Own up to any problems or blocks you might have. Once you get through them, the world is your oyster.
- There is no instant gratification. Work for what you want and soon enough, you'll get it.

Picky, picky.

We all know the old saying, "A woman needs a man like a fish needs a bicycle." Some famous feminist said it and the funny thing is, it's true.

All men want, if I can be crude, is to get laid. Women don't necessarily have to have this. Sure, it's real nice, but is it worth the trouble? Is it worth spending money on new clothes and hairdos and perfume? Is it worth waiting for that damn phone to ring? You have to make yourself worth the trouble. You have to realize that when you first meet, she's not only sizing you up, she's sizing your genes up, too. This is done subconsciously, of course, but she's looking at you as a potential sperm donor. Things race through her mind, subconsciously, "Would he make a good father? Are his genes good? Would he be able to take care of me and a baby if necessary?"

Let's face facts. Once you've ejaculated, you're pretty much done. If the woman becomes pregnant after sex, she's got nine months of hell and then eighteen-plus years of hard labor in front of her. Given that, you'd be picky, too.

One thing you are going to have to do before you begin to transform your life is to stop whining about how difficult women are. We've went through a lot of crap to get here and we're not about to just give it up. A woman's role today is *not* of a subordinate. More than anything she is your genetic superior. Think about it. She can pop a baby out of her vagina. You can't.

Keep in mind that women don't hate men. Just so you'll know, it's not true. I'll say it again: *Women don't hate men.* Women hate the men who have hurt them. So before you call her a "Man hating bitch" remember that she's probably been hurt by one of your kind and is still smarting from it. Don't take it personally.

What we learned:
- Women have the right to be picky.
- All women are not "men hating bitches".
- Try to respect and understand her as much as possible. It's not you who's going to be knocked up, is it?

Three types of men.

Before I say anything else, let me say that I realize that most of you aren't looking for a soul mate. Most of you just want to date a little before finding the right woman. And that's cool. You want a stable of women at your disposal, and, hey, who doesn't? But before you can get your stable, you are going to have to locate this little thing called *confidence*.

A man without confidence is like a martini without an olive. Or nachos without cheese. It just doesn't work. Women want men who have confidence. Women do not want a doormat nor do they want a man they will have to reassure all the time. "Oh, you are too wonderful, honey. Don't worry! I love you!" That's a pain in the butt. Besides, once you're together, it's going to be *you* who has to reassure her most of the time.

I am going to describe the three types of men that women love. As you read, try to take attributes of each of these guys and apply them to yourself. It shouldn't be that hard.

Confident Man:

We all know that some guys have all the luck. They get everything they want and don't even have to work for it. They're born rich or handsome or both. God! How unfair! They're either born knowing how to pick-up women or they've learned from their lothario fathers. These guys can be complete jerks and still have women falling all over them.

You might not be one of these guys. But you can be if you only knew how.

One of the main things that some of these so-called Confident Men have is...well, confidence. They have loads of confidence. I know this guy who is not the best looking guy in the world. He's short and skinny but he has confidence. He has to beat the chicks off him. He knows what to say and when to say it. Why? Because he doesn't care how the chick reacts, he's just looking to goad her a little. Women loved to be teased and he knows how to push those buttons.

Here's his secret: He thinks he's the best there is. He knows in his heart that he's good. He has confidence. He doesn't fear rejection and isn't afraid to approach a woman, nor he is afraid to let one "get away" every once in a while. He knows that another one will appear soon enough. He figures if a woman doesn't want him, then it's her loss. The Confident Man doesn't have to be rich or intelligent or handsome. He just has to be confident. And he's confident because he knows he can give women what they all want: A GOOD TIME! He's a little bit of a mystery and a little bit of a jerk. Not much, but a little just to let her know if she decides to leave him, it won't be long before another one takes her place. This way, he keeps her interested. He knows he's a man and she's a woman and because of that, he never beats around the bush.

He never stares at the woman he's trying to woo the entire time. He looks around, but from time to time, he stares her directly in the eye, allowing a small smile to play on his lips. He also lets his eyes dart to her cleavage every once in a while and he also sips his drink while he's talking. He's always on and for that reason, she's usually turned on by him.

Another way to look at it: He's laid-back. This does not mean he's cocky. He's *always* a gentleman.

Once you learn more about women, you can start pushing their buttons but in a good way. Women love for men to pay attention to them. But there has to be something special about that man who's doing the paying. What is that special something? As I've said before it's just confidence. That's all it is! This shouldn't be a secret but for some reason, it is. You have to have confidence to walk up to her and to offer to buy her a drink. You have to have confidence as you're talking to her—the "She should be glad I'm taking the time" kind of confidence. And you will have it in time.

In review: Learn to be more confident. Learn to be a little flirty once you've got a chick's attention. Learn how to push her buttons in the good way. Learn to let her go if she chooses and never let it bother you if she disses you. So what if it doesn't work out? Move on to the next woman.

The (elusive) Bad Boy:

I've never seen the big deal but a lot of women want the Bad Boy. They think that they will get to see the loving side of this guy, that he will be a teddy bear and that only *they* will crack his tough exterior to see the scared little boy inside that they can shape and mold and, obviously, heal.

And, that my friends, is why women like the bad boy. He's a challenge. In my opinion, he's a pain in the butt. And I say this because most times he's going to be a jerk. Women may get their bad boys but they also get a lot of pain to go along with him. And usually, they get a cheater to go along with their pain. The funny thing about this is, if they are successful in reforming the Bad Boy, they usually find that they don't want him anymore. He's no longer interesting.

You don't have to be a bad boy to get women. The thing that bad boys do that rest of you don't is that they hold back.

They don't fawn over women. They'll give a girl a good once-over, then stare her directly in the eye. This makes her see that he's aggressive enough to do something but for some reason, he's holding back. Then her little mind goes to racing. *Why isn't he coming to me? Why isn't he doing anything? Don't I look hot tonight?* They don't realize that because he's a Bad Boy, they've got to go to him. Bad Boys don't chase women. Women chase Bad Boys.

Learn that lesson from the Bad Boys. Just hold back. Unless she's a bitch, she will come to you. The great thing is, even if she is a bitch, she'll come on over anyway. *Why is this dude checking me out and not doing anything about it?* Believe me, she wants to know why.

Of course, if you don't have a bunch of tattoos and a Harley parked outside, what are you going to do if she comes over? What are you going to give her? A ride in your Honda? A free drink? Women are attracted to Bad Boys because they think there's something else *there.* Who knows what it may be, but that's why they get so riled up. Of course, realistically, women are attracted to bad boys because they know they are going to take them on a wild ride of some kind—preferably in bed. But once the ride's over, there's a lot of pain to sort through.

You can be a Bad Boy without being bad. All you have to do is take what bad boys do—treat women like meat—and tweak it. You can give them those looks without raping them with your eyes. You can be bad in bed but a total gentleman otherwise.

In review: Bad Boys act like they have something on women. They are elusive. Act like that and you've got her.

The Smart Guy:

You want to be one of these guys. Here's what they do:

- Smart guys watch dating shows and pay attention to their friends' dating stories. Let the other guy make the mistake and you learn the lesson.
- Smart guys know when to pull back.
- Smart guys let the chicks know that he notices them and then he makes them wait a little while before he approaches them.
- Smart guys watch shows on human behavior on the Discovery Channel and find out how we tick.
- Smart guys watch James Bond films and learn a thing or two about the art of seduction and tease from the master.
- Smart guys take notes and study women with diligence.
- Smart guys put forth the effort and know if they do, they can get something back.
- Smart guys dress nice, smell nice and are always courteous to a woman even if she disses him. Smoothness is a must.

So, take elements from all three of these men. Take the confidence from the Confident Man, combine it with the elusive nature of the Bad Boy and study it like a Smart Guy. By combining these factors, you will find your own personal pattern and comfort level and then work it. If you can do this, then you won't have a worry in the world. You won't need loads of money or looks. You can be you but with more confidence and know-how. You can be Mr. Joe Average who's a little bit of a mystery and a touch of the bad boy every girl desires.

But the biggest thing is to have confidence. Once you know you can ask a chick out without falling all over yourself, and that she should be happy you are, you'll have no problem.

There, you got it. *That's* the big secret these guys have. You just have to learn to use it to *your* advantage. But, alas, that skill will come in time.

What we learned:
- There are three types of men: The Confident Man, the Bad Boy and the Smart Guy.
- Combine elements of all three and become a master at seduction and tease.

Myths.

There are a lot of myths floating around out there about this and about that. Let's go through a few of them, shall we?

Myth: *You can make anyone fall in love with you.*
Truth: This is absolute bullcrap. Of course, after they've known you for a while, sure, maybe. But if you and she don't have the right chemistry, no amount of anything is going to make her fall for you. Do you know that smell has a lot to do with people falling in love? We cover ourselves up with colognes and perfumes so our natural pheromones can't shine through. My advice? Take a good bath, wash everything and use just a touch of cologne. See if it works.

Myth: *With the right moves, you can get laid by any girl.*
Truth: Again, absolute bullcrap. You may be one helluva guy, but not every woman in the whole world is going to want to have sex with you. I don't care if you were her shoulder to cry on or shelter from the storm outside. I don't care how much you spent on her. She will either like you enough to let you get into her pants or she won't. In fact, she doesn't have to do anything. You're the man; you're the one who's supposed to take charge. And, even if you do get lucky, she could still diss you after it's all said and done. Love's a bitch, ain't it?

Myth: *Learning body language secrets will let you know if a girl likes you.*

Truth: Yeah, but what if you're in a dark club? If a girl likes you—really likes you—she isn't going to let you get away if—IF!—you give her a signal that you're interested. Trust me, the best way to see if a chick likes you is to approach her. Women are just as confused and just as nervous about approaching you as you are them. They're looking for signs, too. And what if both of you misread the signs? Well, you're both out of luck, aren't you? If she isn't interested, then it's over and you can move onto the next one.

Myth: *You have to be rich to get girls nowadays.*
Truth: Women like money but guys with money are usually jerks. Sure, they might let them buy them stuff, but will they fall in love with someone who treats them like dirt? Probably not. Besides, do you really want to have to buy her love?

Myth: *Girls play hard to get.*
Truth: This one is true and it's probably one of the stupider things girls do. It's very frustrating to guys. However, it's not going to stop, so you need to learn how to deal with it. One of the reasons girls do this is that they believe that you, the male, are the natural born aggressor. Think about our hunting and gathering days. Women gathered, men hunted. Men were out all day killing wild animals and bringing the chow into camp. If you didn't do it back then, you might not have to do it now. But, alas, you did, so you have to.

It's not going to change. No matter what, women want men who will confidently approach them. Women don't like to chase men. It makes them feel sleazy. This does not mean that you have to hound a chick. This means that you should approach her and start talking. Nature should take its course after that initial meeting.

The point is, some of this stuff is true, on a very superficial level. As I've said, what works for one, won't work for another—*ever!* Knowing how women work is going to give you the edge. However, trying to outguess her or play tricks on her or even using hypnosis will never work. Knowing why she does what she does is better than trying to outwit her. Don't ever try to one-up a woman. She will have your balls in no time flat. Remember she's got what you want. She doesn't really need you.

There are a few universal truths to what women really want from men. Most say that a nice smile, nice clothes and a clean body do the trick. Does he have to be handsome? No, not necessarily. But he does have to have a personality. There has to be *something* there for them to latch onto. If you give her a cardboard cutout of what you think she wants, she's going to see right through you. No amount of money or good clothing or pheromones are gonna save you. You were born with a distinct personality which you should never try to change. If you use it right, you can land the girl of your dreams. And by using it right, I mean, being man enough to be yourself. And if you give her yourself with those three elements I spoke of in the previous chapter, you are home-free.

What we learned:
- Most myths about dating are bullcrap.
- Stop thinking about myths and start concentrating on improving yourself.
- Most people who rely on myths are game players.

Use what you've got.

The best advice I, or anyone else for that matter, can give you is to use what you've got. Use what you've got and don't be afraid to do it. Maybe you're not the best looking guy but you have a big dick. That's always a crowd pleaser. Maybe you're cute but you have a crappy job. Maybe you get tongue-tied around women but you're working on a novel. Women eat that stuff right up. You're an artist? Hey, you've just written your own ticket. Maybe you're in some stupid garage band. Man, why are you reading this book? Women don't care if you're talented or not. As long as you're behind some instrument, you're sure to get laid sooner or later.

The point is to think of what you have. Right now. Stop and think. Okay. So you've got it. You can fix her computer if it tears up or you can change the oil in her car. Whatever it is, use it, work it to your advantage.

On the other hand, there is this thing called *Artificial Coolness* where some people act like they're a lot cooler than they are. Or maybe they pretend to have a lot of money or a cool job or whatever. Let me tell you one thing, chicks can and will see right through that. Never, ever pretend to be something you're not. No one likes a fake of any kind. Don't be a phony. It will come right back and bite you. And it hurts a lot when it does.

All you have to do is act like yourself. You have to accept yourself first before you can ask anyone else to accept you. So what if you're not where you wanted to be financially? So what if you haven't done the things you wanted to do? You will, in time. Just don't pretend to be something you're not.

Women are also interested in guys who do want to improve themselves and do more with their lives. The point is that you have to have something to offer a woman. You just have to do a little soul searching and find it. Everybody has something and if you can't find anything, you're not looking hard enough. If you have nothing to offer, then you're not going to get anything in return. What you give is what you get. Find out what you have and then get ready to offer it up. Got nothing but the shirt on your back? Prepare to spend your life alone. At least you know what you're up against.

You might even want to consider this. Lower your expectations. If the model doesn't want anything to do with you, why not go with the normal chick who hasn't been surgically enhanced? Sure, I know men want beautiful women with big tits who can cook. And women want men who are rich, good looking and have a great sense of humor. No wonder we're all miserable. So why always go for the women you probably don't have a chance with? I'm not saying to date a woman with rotten teeth who is five hundred pounds overweight. I'm saying, don't overlook the good women out there who aren't built like a Barbie doll.

All of us have some flaws and most of us don't look like movie stars. So what if she has small tits? Small tits look great when that shirt comes off. Some say that more than a handful is a waste, so don't knock 'em till you try 'em. And you're not going to be dating her tits anyway. You're dating *her.* Accepting and loving every part of her and what she has to offer is one of the best things you can do. Accept her and her flaws because she's going to do the same thing for you.

None of us are perfect, thank God. As with real beauty, real ugliness is rare. Today, it's all about the looks. But most of us look pretty good already. So do yourself a favor and stop comparing chicks with other chicks. Stop comparing them with models and Playmates and actresses. This is a very immature thing to do. You're not in junior high anymore. They are just like you: Ordinary people. And, for God's sake, if you have a ranking game with your buddies— the one where you rate chicks on a scale of one to ten—stop that. That is so crass and rude it's unbelievable. If a chick catches you doing it, you are toast. And you know what? The only guys who do that are the ones who don't have a chance in hell with any of the chicks they're ranking. It's nothing more than a way for them to put these girls down. Shame on them! And if you do it, shame on you! Or, look at it like this: what would you think if a woman did this to you?

What we learned:
- Use what you got.
- Never rate women on a scale of 1-10.

It's all about the Benjamins.

It's true. In order to turn yourself into a dating machine, you are going to have to spend some bread. And when you get a girl, expect to spend even more. You don't have to be rich, but you need some cash so you don't come off looking like a cheapskate.

Now listen, this is extremely important: *Women hate and despise cheap men.* They will run in the other direction when confronted with one. No woman wants to be with any guy who won't spend a few bucks on her. If you can't afford a few dinners out and a bouquet of flowers from time to time, you might as well hang it up now.

So what if you don't have any cash right now? You got a job, don't you? (You better.) Right now, this minute, start a "Dating Fund". Put a little money back every week for dating. Put it in a safe place (like your sock drawer) and leave it alone. Once you're ready to go out there, you've got the cash you need and, believe me, you will need it. Women are expensive.

Women want to be pampered. If they know you're willing to spend a little on them, more than likely, they'll give you a chance to do a little something-something in the bedroom. It sounds like you're paying for it, doesn't it? Well, you're not. You're just trying to impress her that you're the kind of guy that she wants to spend more time with. This is the way it works in the real world.

That wasn't so bad, was it? Well, this is.

One thing that bugs me is the Dutch Treat. You know what that is, don't you? Where you and your date split the cost of dinner straight down the middle. How tacky and horrible is that?!

This may have worked in college but let me tell you, she's not so understanding once you get a job. You're no longer a poor student to her. You're a cheapskate.

"Here, let's see…you had the manicotti and I had the prime rib…"

Thank the good Lord above, but I have never had a guy do that to me. One of my friends wasn't so lucky. She told me, "Dinner was over and we were getting along great. I was actually beginning to like this guy. The check came and the waitress put it in the middle of the table. I just glanced at it and smiled a little, not thinking, you know, that we were going to go Dutch or anything. I mean, *he* asked me out, not the other way around. Well, he had other ideas. He started playing with his watch and I realized he had a calculator on it! This jerk split the check down to the very last cent! We even split the tip! You don't have to ask if I ever saw him again, do you?"

Just so you'll know, she didn't.

Women like to be treated like they are somebody special. Are you willing to treat her like that? I mean, don't embarrass yourself. If you can't afford to take her out, or are just too damned cheap to part with a dollar, stay home and watch TV.

So, even if she insists, do *not* let her pay. Let me say that again in case you've got wax in your ears: *Do not ever let her pay for anything!* If you make her pay, this tells her that you're not really interested or you're just a dork who doesn't know any better. It makes her feel like crap and not at all special. Maybe this is a catch-22 but who said love was easy?

When a man is a cheapskate and doesn't want to pay for dinner, this tells a woman a lot of things. It tells her that if they got married, he would be the type of guy who asks why she needs so many shoes. And also, this sends a pretty clear signal that he can't afford to help her raise a family or even buy a house. Or that he'd be one of those fathers who makes his kids pick up cans off the side of the road.

Not a prospect many women want. Hell, she can afford her own dinner, you know? If she has to pay, why would she need you?

This is not to say that you should go bankrupt in order to become a dating machine. In fact, if you do stuff that is out of your price range, your next date can't be at Burger King. Anything less than what you did on the first date will be a letdown.

So what can you do? Find stuff that's in your price range. Also, start your fund and keep a few dollars around in case you get lucky and get a date. Being prepared doesn't mean being cheap. However, if you can't afford a nice dinner, you are going to have to get creative and work a little harder. It'll be a pain in the butt, but worth it in the long run.

Places and/or things you might do on the cheap:

- You can cook for her at your place. Steaks don't cost that much.
- You can meet her in the park for a picnic. You can buy finger foods at the grocery store.
- You can see the matinee show at the movies or theatre.
- You can attend free outdoor concerts.
- You can window shop.
- You can write her poems about the lovely color of her hair.

- If you're a guitarist, you can play for her.
- You can go for long drives in your car.

If she likes you bunches, she isn't really going to care *where* you take her as long as you're a gentleman and pay for everything. But remember, if you're a cheap bastard, you're never going to get to see the inside of her bedroom. It's like this, dude: If you don't pay, she ain't gonna let you play. And I bet you're sick of playing with yourself.

What we learned:
- It's never a good idea to be cheap.
- Never ask a woman to go "Dutch".
- You don't have to be rich to date. Find inexpensive alternatives.

Mind your manners.

Your mother should have taught you better. Apparently, she didn't. That's why I'm here. Women like men with manners. Bad manners spell bad boyfriend. Simply put, when you look at her, you're looking at a good time in the sack. When she looks at you, she's usually looking for a potential boyfriend. Even if she says she's just there to get laid, she's looking for a mate. Or at least a regular hook-up. And she doesn't want anything to do with you if you're bad boyfriend potential. I mean, why should she bother at all?

Bad boyfriend forgets to clean himself. He's weird and smelly and just plain bad news. You want to be good boyfriend. The upside? Good boyfriend always gets laid.

So what can you do? It's pretty easy to have good manners. Most of it is just common sense. Go ask Miss Manners if you have to. Watch some Martha Stewart or read a book on etiquette.

But there are a few little things that you should be aware of. And the most important thing you will read in this book or ever be told is: *Hold the damned door open for her.*

I know when a guy doesn't do this, it spells loser to me. It's like he's getting ahead of himself and doesn't even know I'm there. I think, *How good is this guy going to be in bed if he isn't considerate enough to open the door for me?*

Here are a few other things you should know:
- Again, open the door for her. Get a little ahead of her, open it and then let her enter first, following

close behind, but not too close where you'll step on her heels.

- Open her car door *first*. Let her get inside, shut it and then go to your side. This spells gentleman and consideration. And that racks up major points with chicks.

- Never, ever, ever slam the door in her face. Even if you're mad at her.

- If you're going to a nice restaurant, pull the chair out for her and wait until she sits before you sit. How easy is that? Not that easy because I have witnessed many guys just plunking down before the chick even makes it to the table. Whenever I see this, I always think, *jerk*. So does she.

- Don't chew gum.

- If you smoke, wait until after. Before you start puffing, test the waters as to her attitude towards smoking. If she doesn't smoke, she may not want anything to do with you. Hide it or quit.

- Never burp. A girl I know told me, "I was out with this guy and out of nowhere, he burped. Not a little, oh-excuse-me kind of burp, but a loud raunchy burp. A stinky one! And the kicker is he didn't ask to be excused." Why would anyone do that? Beats me, but if you do it, plan on going home alone. Of course, once you start seeing someone on a regular basis, you might accidentally let out a burp or fart. Once you do, either apologize or laugh it off. We all burp and fart. Just not in the first, tentative stages.

- A word on cursing. I don't think you should jump right into it until you've felt her out a little. She could be one of those chicks who rarely curses and just doesn't see a need for "such" language.

This doesn't mean she's necessarily a prude—it might be a good indicator, though—but it's a good idea to wait until she uses the first curse word. Regardless of how much she curses, don't overdo it and get crude. Remember, you're not around the boys. I know this is a double standard but she might see her cursing as sassy and yours as threatening. She may have been brought up in a family where men don't curse around women. There are some of those out there, you know?

- Don't throw a mad, hissy fit even if you stump your toe or catch your dick in your pants. (If you do, I do feel sorry for you.) Be a man about it and suffer in silence.

- If she does something to piss you off—chances are, at some point, she will—just grimace and let it go. You can call a buddy up later and vent. But, at first, do not throw a temper tantrum in front of her. It spells future wife beater.

- You're a bastard if... You get her drunk off her butt and take advantage of her. If you do this, you will rot in hell! That is so sleazy.

- Do not correct her spelling or pronunciation. Don't correct her! It's a one way ticket to hell! If she makes a jerk out of herself, let her. Or smile and think about how cute it is when she mispronounces something.

- Don't ever give her fashion tips. You are a dead man if you do. Remember, she's going to see you as a project regardless of whether you are or not. So nothing you say regarding fashion will have any validity. (Most women believe they're all fashion aficionados.)

- Don't ever ask if she's a real blonde, otherwise, you have zero chance of finding out for yourself, which, everyone knows, is much more fun.
- Don't ever ask about her shaving habits. (You know I'm not talking about her legs, don't you?)
- Don't ever disrespect her.
- Don't ever hit her! Otherwise, you might find yourself in jail.
- Don't ever call or think she's a whore if you've just slept with her. If you think stuff like that, you've got issues and need to seek help ASAP!
- Don't ask, don't tell. Past sexual experiences should be kept in the past. More than likely she is probably more experienced than you want her to be and probably more experienced than you. Remember, she's been around guys like you for years. Hope she's had a good teacher and forget about it. When it eventually comes up, just be happy that you're with a seasoned veteran. Virginity is highly overrated.
- Don't ever get her name wrong. Ask twice if you have to and memorize it, even ask her to spell it in case you're having trouble. If you pronounce it wrong, she will correct you. Take notes. (She is.)

These are just a few things you should know before you undertake dating. The more you know, the better off you'll be. In dating, it is *always* about the woman. Hard truth, but if you're too selfish and self-centered to learn this, you might always be alone. This is what all good daters know. Sure, you can have fun, too, but getting off on the wrong foot by forgetting something as small as opening the door for her spells disaster.

I know what you're thinking: *Why does stuff like this matter so much to chicks?* Who knows why? But it does. Always remember that it is you who is romancing her. It is you who is showing yourself to her to see if she likes. It is you who is on display. Play your cards right and you'll never get rid of her. And then you can be in charge a little.

Another important thing to do is to grow up. Immaturity won't cut it. Grow a pair for God's sake! Partying-and-having-a-good-time guy might go home with the bar slut, but he's not going to ever develop a real relationship.

What we learned:

- Mind your manners. All women love men who have good manners.

Teeth.

When was the last time you had your teeth cleaned, or for that matter, X-rayed? (Every six months is when you're *supposed* to do it.) If it's been a while, know that your choppers are one of the first things chicks will notice and that's because they know a man who takes good care of his teeth will also take good care of them.

If you take care of these little things, she's going to have no reason to turn you down. More importantly, she's going to have no reason to try and change you. Yeah, right. She will always try to change you because that's what women do. But the point is, don't give her anything to start with. Make her work to change you. Improve on yourself first before she even gets in the picture and she'll wonder how she got so lucky. She'll tell her girlfriends, "I don't know why, but there's nothing wrong with this guy! I mean, can there be *nothing* wrong with him? His teeth are good, he has great manners and he always holds the door open for me. Am I just being paranoid?"

Now, take a good look at your teeth in the mirror. Are they stained? Are some missing? If so, get an appointment with a dentist and get all that nasty work done. You want to keep your teeth in tip-top shape, otherwise, you'll have to get dentures on down the road.

It's also a good idea to whiten your teeth. You can start by using whitening toothpaste. If you've got the cash, have the dentist do it. If you can afford it, get your choppers fixed even if you've only got a few snaggles here and there. Some women don't mind teeth that are slightly crooked but if they're so bad you look like an extra in an hillbilly movie, please do yourself a favor and get this done.

You may be saying, *Is there anything women don't notice?* And the answer is, no. there's not. Good luck to you, though.

What we learned:
- Everything is important to women and that includes your teeth. Be sure to get your pearly whites in tip-top shape.

Be prepared.

There are a few universal truths to what all women want. Ready for them?

What she wants:
- For you to be perfect.
- To change you. (She will try.)
- Marriage. I don't care what she says, she usually wants marriage. All women do. The only exception to this is if she's been married before or burned by man. Or if she's a lesbian and we all know lesbians only want to marry one another.
- Babies. This is one of her major life goals. (An exception: she already has babies and doesn't want any more.)

You have been warned. Do not proceed if any of this makes you break into hives.

Bad reputation.

You might not give a damn about your bad rep—in fact, you're probably proud of it—but she sure as hell cares about hers. She doesn't want anything to mess with her chances of getting a good guy and, perhaps eventually, a good husband. She also doesn't want you to think she's some kind of slut. Even if she is easy, she doesn't want anyone *else* to think it.

I once knew a guy who had a really good first date with a chick and then he jumped the gun and asked her, "So can I stay over at your place tonight?" And he wondered why she turned cold after that. I told him, "It's really simple, stupid. One of the biggest dating rules is that you never ask a chick if you can stay at her place. Whatever chance you had just went down the tubes. Why? Because, after you say something like that, she thinks you think she's a cheap ho and that makes her feel bad about herself."

Don't ever invite yourself to her place. Ever, even if you're getting "vibes" that she wants you to stay over. If she wants this, she will let your know. There will be *no* shadow of doubt. She doesn't want you to think that she's "easy" or "cheap" and if you ask this dumb question, that's precisely what you're telling her you think of her. You're telling her that all you're interested in is sex.

Believe me, once you let a woman know this, she will turn ice cold. It's true. Yes, it *is*. It might not make sense, but I know women think in these terms. Even if she's forty years old, she's still concerned with getting a bad reputation. Always wait for an invite! *Always!* Never, ever invite yourself up to some chick's pad! It will get you a one-way ticket to nowhere.

Now you can invite her to *your* pad, but do it nicely, "I have some really good gin at my place. Want to come up for a drink? You know, just a drink. I would love to keep talking to you."

I know that your mind is going to be on sex the entire evening, but never let *her* know it is. And when you invite her, don't think you're going to get lucky.

On the other hand, if she thinks you're not that interested in sex, she's going to want to know why. *Why doesn't he desire me? I've got to figure this guy out.* Coming on too strong with a lady is going to get you a ticket home— alone. Holding back and letting her come to you might just be your ticket to a night of wild monkey sex.

Let me reiterate. The more you act like you're not interested in sex, the stronger she will come on to you. Don't ever show that's all you're interested in—we all know it is— until she comes to you. Don't ever assume that she wants it. She might, but if you tell her you know what she's thinking, she's going to turn cold.

What if you do screw up and do something like the idiot I mentioned above? Claim stupidity. Tell her that you're drunk. That you didn't mean it. Tell her you were only joking. Laugh it off. Say you're sorry and if you still have a chance, she'll let you know. And move on to another subject quickly. Women do have long memories but if you brush it off, she may brush it off as well because she'll be embarrassed. And the reason she'll be embarrassed is because she'll think *she's* the one jumping the gun.

One of the most important things you can do is to *think before you speak.* She's keeping score, believe me.

What we learned:

- Women do care about their reputations.
- Women don't want you or anyone else to think they're a cheap ho.
- Never invite yourself to her place.
- Invite her to your place only if you get the vibe she's digging you.

Your music.

If you have the opportunity to bring a good looking girl home, you need some good tunes to help woo her. Take a good, hard look at your CD collection. Teenybopper music? *Kenny G?!* Oh, good Lord! Hide those CDs or throw them away, which is even better. Get some rock-n-roll—Stones or Led Zeppelin or something with a little soul. Women usually love oldies and Otis Redding is always, always good. Women swoon when they hear him. (I know I do.) You might also want to get some Patsy Cline. I know, it's country, but Patsy is just so good. You should already have some Dean Martin and Frank Sinatra in your collection. You do, right?

Remember, good music is the best music to set the stage. Get some music that shows you're a suave, sophisticated guy, not some frat-boy or axe-murderer. If you don't know where to start, that geek in the record store will.

What we learned:
- Keep some good music around that will set the stage and let her know how cool you are.
- If you don't have any good music, get some.
- If you don't know where to start, start with the classics: Dean, Frank, Elvis, Beatles, etc.
- If you still don't know where to start, ask the geek at the record store. (Make sure he's not wearing a Metallica t-shirt, though.)

Me Tarzan. You Jane.

No. No. No.

This may work in the movies but in real life, women rarely respond to a cave man/Tarzan mentality or any of that crap. If you try to woo her by beating your fists on your chest, expect her to call the cops. I know I would. *This guy is crazy!* You may be bigger, stronger and faster than she is, but she doesn't give a flying fig. (Neither does anyone else.)

You're not a male chauvinist pig, are you? If so, you are going to have a hard time hooking up. If you think that a woman's place is in the kitchen, why are you even bothering? Women expect and demand respect. If you aren't willing to give it to her, go buy a blow-up doll to be your girlfriend. She won't contradict you. And she's always available.

Another thing: Never alpha male a woman! By this I mean, don't push her around and don't try to "control" her in any way. I have seen this happen and it just makes me cringe. Never try to get the upper hand. I would hope that you would want to be on equal-footing with a chick and she you. But if you try to show your manliness by pushing her around, you just blew your chances.

Trust is the key. You have to let her know that if you two get behind closed doors you're not going to do anything bad. You are a lot bigger than her and she *has* to feel safe with you. You have to be trustworthy and the thing is, you either are or you aren't. Most people can pick up on this trait pretty quickly. If she gets bad vibes of any kind, she's gone.

It's a protective measure. Do what you have to do to let her know she can trust you. Building trust takes time but know that it is a very necessary step if you want to succeed with women.

What we learned:
- Me Tarzan, you Jane never works.
- Never alpha male a female, i.e., never push her around.
- If you're a male chauvinist pig, you need to change your attitude.

Never let her see you cry like a baby.

If you ask me, there is way too much male crying going on these days. You can't turn on the TV without seeing it. It's all over the movies. I mean, if something tragic has happened, by all means, cry your little heart out. But if you just found out your favorite TV show is going off the air, don't do it in front of her.

This is one of the myths that I think started in the seventies—the "All women like men who aren't afraid to cry" myth. Now every man out there is crying. You can't turn the TV on without seeing one blubbering away. And usually they're crying for stupid reasons, because they haven't been sensitive *enough* or something just as mundane. Truthfully, this makes us look like a nation of crybabies.

While it may be true that women like men to be a bit sensitive, they do not like crybabies. Remember, just like you have opinions on how women should act, they too have opinions on how men should act.

Life's a bitch.

On the other hand, expect *her* to cry. Be the shoulder she cries on. Women love to cry, it makes them feel good, it's cathartic. Just keep in mind that she's allowed to cry because she's a girl.

Also, God forbid if you should start talking about your feelings on the first few dates. Keep in mind that, at first, she won't care about your feelings. Feelings about the world and the beautiful sun and all that should be kept in check at first. Remember, she's looking for a man, but not an ultra-sensitive one. She doesn't want you to be soft. Therefore, until you've dated for a while, refrain from talking about your feelings. It's tacky and just a little bit creepy.

On the other hand, if she asks you to open up, open up—a little. Give her a story from your childhood that you remember fondly. *Don't* tell her about the time you were beaten up on the school bus.

One last thing, if you want to share your poetry, please don't. You should know why.

What we learned:
- Cry only if something tragic happens, not at the beautiful sunset.
- Share your "feelings" only after you've been seeing someone for a while.
- If you do open up, give only a little—preferably funny—story. Don't bore her with tiny details.
- If she cries, be her shoulder.
- Poetry is a big no-no.

Hey, doughboy!

You have to be stronger than she is. If she could easily kick your butt, what does she need you for? You have to have something to offer her and being strong is a biggie. Being a doughboy isn't.

Have you noticed the new American male physique? Many of you seem to look like—and I'm not going to be nice here—but all of you look like doughboys. All of you look like the Pillsbury Doughboy! What the hell are you eating? Do you *ever* get up off the couch? Even the guys in rock bands have it now. Do you think that this is attractive to the opposite sex?

Well, it's not.

I'm hoping and praying you don't look like a doughboy. If you do, face up to it and get ready to whip your butt into shape. *But,* you whine, *I don't wanna!* Fine by me. You don't wanna get laid, either, do you?

Women spend so much time keeping themselves in shape its unreal. We spend hours jogging and lifting weights and thinking about that damned piece of chocolate cake we passed up at lunch. Why do we do it? Because we want to look good for the opposite sex. And then you men just let yourselves go. It's hardly fair when you get right down to it. Let me ask you this: Who the hell told you men that you don't have to expend any effort on your appearance? Who said that was okay? What makes you any different? I am taking a stand now. If you men don't start getting into shape, we women should stop, too.

Scary thought, isn't it? All the beautiful women walking around looking like...like *so fat.* You will have to resort to a fantasy of an island far away that has a harem of beautiful, in-shape women on it. And that's all it's gonna be, too—a fantasy.

Some of you might be saying, *But looks don't matter.* Like hell they don't! The only way they don't matter is if you're a multi-millionaire with a Stetson hat propped on your head and a Caddy parked on the corner.

Face it. Face it now. You need to look good. Looking good is the best way to attract women. If you look like a doughboy, they won't want anything to do with you. In fact, they won't want to be seen out in public with you.

Women want someone they can be attracted to, physically and emotionally, because after you get together, women take on a more responsible role in the household. They want to know they can take time off to have a kid. If you've got a big gut hanging over your jeans, she's going to have to worry about your health. She wants someone who can keep up with her. She wants a man in good shape.

They invented gyms for a reason, didn't they? So, start working out. If you can afford it, hire a personal trainer. Tell them what part of your body you want to get in shape. (Nothing says L-U-S-T like a good set of pecs.) You can afford at least one session. Ask them to show you the basic exercises that will get you in shape and that you can do at home. An added bonus is that there are tons of honeys around in tight-fitting workout gear.

Besides that, a simple jog can do wonders. You do not have to invest in expensive exercise equipment. Free weights are relatively inexpensive and there are many simple exercises you can do with them to get in shape. You can also get lots of exercise ideas from fitness magazines and on the web. Do a little research and fit it into your schedule.

Everyone has at least twenty to thirty minutes a day to exercise.

If you have over 20 pounds to lose, consider going on a diet. It doesn't have to be anything extreme, just cut down on your food intake and no beer! *No beer!* Stop crying! (We've already discussed that!) You can have a beer after you get rid of your flab.

If you have *less* than 20 pounds to lose, try this: Eat whatever you like, but only eat half. And cut down on your starches (bread, pasta but not fruits and veggies!). It is necessary to look your best. The better shape you're in, the more likely you're going to hook up. And you will have a better chance of getting laid if you look good.

What we learned:
- If you're overweight, lose it.
- Women love hard bodies. Turn yourself into a hard body—but not a bodybuilder—and you shouldn't have any trouble hooking up.

Sharp dressed man.

Pick up your purses, girls, we're going shopping!

Take a good hard look at yourself. How old is that shirt you're wearing? What are those things on your feet? You call those shoes? *But*, you say, *they're comfortable.* If I hear one more man tell me he wears what he wears because of comfort I am going to blow a gasket. What does comfort have to do with anything? After you break them in, any pair of shoes you buy will be comfortable.

I can always tell a single man these days because of the way he dresses. If he looks like crap, that means a woman hasn't gotten a hold of him yet and straightened him out. You have to dress well. This is *hugely* important to women. If you don't care about how you look, why should she care at all?

Women spend a huge amount of money on new clothing. If you knew how much, you would appreciate them all the more. And you would wonder how they can afford it. Two words: Credit cards. Women are going in debt to look nice for you. That's how important it is to them. They put all this time into the way they look and you think you can get away with dressing in an old t-shirt and jeans or, God *forbid*, sweatpants? Nuh uh. You think just because you're a great guy she's going to pick you out of a crowd even if you dress like a slob? Well, she might pick you out, but she's just going to think to herself, "Man, what a dork!"

You don't want to be a fixer-upper!

If this upsets you, then stop trying to get a woman. Don't change. They don't care if you're interested or not. Don't say, "Well, they're too superficial." So what? You base first impressions on looks, don't you? I know you do because everyone does. You're going to notice the pretty woman in a tight dress with the spectacular boobs before you notice the wallflower in the corner dressed in overalls. Right?

You say, *It should all be about the inside, the inner beauty.* What a crock. People mate with one another because of attraction, physical and chemical. Besides, how can they see the inner beauty if they can't get past the Member's Only jacket? If you dress like a dork, expect to be treated as such.

I've seen lots of nice looking guys who dress like dorks. They don't have a clue as to why no one wants to hook up with them. It might not be "fair" but that's how it really is. Chicks may be too nice to come out and tell you they didn't want anything to do with you because you look like an extra from *Revenge of the Nerds*. But then again, they won't go out with you either. You don't want to jeopardize your chances of getting lucky because you were dressed sloppy. Sometimes, all chicks will give you is *one glance*. That first impression is very crucial. If they don't like what they see, they are not going to give you the time of day.

Let's go over a few of those atrocities in your closet. This is stuff that needs to be weeded out. If you have to keep it, never wear it when you are trying to pick up women.

Get rid of this crap:

- *The golf shirt.* I hate golf! You know why? Because now everyone and their mother are wearing these God-awful things. A golf shirt is *not* a good shirt to wear. It is not a good indicator that you have any style whatsoever. If you're anything like most men, you probably got one free somewhere.

- *Team shirts.* Oh, brother. Do you people think that if you wear a shirt with "your" team's logo that makes you part of the team? Newsflash: It doesn't! Never, ever wear a shirt with your favorite team's logo on it. I don't care how big a fan you are or if they just won the superbowl, don't do it.

- *Baseball caps.* How old are you? I mean, really. Sure, wear a baseball cap to...*say*...a baseball game! Why is that thing on your head every time you hit the door? What are you trying to hide? If you show up for a date with a baseball hat turned around backwards, don't be surprised if she shoves it up your butt.

- *Shorts.* I was recently in London watching the local news and they had a reporter on the streets asking men (mostly American) why they were wearing shorts. It's, like, a crime over there or something. Make it a crime over here. Help start a trend!

- *Sneakers.* Why? Why? *WHY!* Why are you still wearing sneakers? *Seinfeld* went off the air years ago! Do hard-soled shoes hurt your little feet? You poor thing. Why don't you just stay home and forget about it? If you go out in sneakers, you might as well.

- *Sebago's or "dock" shoes.* You don't still have a pair of these, do you? You do know they went out of style about twenty years ago, don't you? If you have a pair of Sebago's, please do the rest of the world a favor and *throw them out.*

Fashion dos and don'ts:

- *Pants:* Flat-fronted slacks are the best. They are also the most stylish. I don't have to tell you these pants need to be in a solid color, do I? Okay, buy pants in a solid color. No stripes or plaids allowed. Black, gray, and khaki are the best colors.

- *Shirts.* Solid color button-down shirts in a good cotton material. You can also find some that are cotton/poly blended that look great. No crazy stripes or patterns. Just plain shirts that will go well with your pants. Also, Hawaiian shirts should be reserved for special occasions. Like when you go to Hawaii.

- *Sweaters.* Lightweight material in solid colors. A crew-neck or v-neck is good and should always be worn with a white t-shirt underneath. (Think Gap or Banana Republic.)

- *Belts.* Belt color must match shoe color. Hopefully, neither will be in white.

- *Undershirts.* White, all cotton t-shirts that should be unstained. Wear them under all shirts. You can also wear those wife-beater shirts under your shirts. As long as you're not a wife-beater, that is. (Wash them separately and use a little bleach which will keep them looking whiter for longer.)

- *Underwear.* Now, I know a few of you are going to get your feathers up about this—why I don't know—but let's get it over and done with. If you get lucky enough to worry about a lovely lady seeing your skivvies, wear boxers or boxer briefs. Tighty whities won't get it. She will laugh at you if you strip down and stand there in a pair. Maybe not to your face but imagine the things she's going to tell her girlfriends. Yeah. She'll tell them *everything.* And if you own a pair of Speedo-type skivvies, I just worry about you. Going commando isn't recommended, either.

- *Socks.* No white socks unless you are wearing jeans or khakis. Colored—black, brown, tan— socks for all other pants. And no argyles! Any socks with pills on them or holes should be thrown out.

- *Holes.* In fact, anything that has holes the manufacturer didn't put in should be thrown out as well as anything that is stained or ragged. If you have any doubt about something, throw it out.

- *Coats.* A good leather coat—in black or dark brown but preferably in black—is a good investment and can be worn with anything. Make sure it is in a classic style and if you buy a motorcycle jacket, be sure to have a motorcycle. (Note that these jackets are not recommended.) You might also want to get a wool or wool-blended jacket that zips or buttons down. These are good in black and should hit around the hip area. Please do not ever wear a duster coat of any kind unless you are mounting a horse.

- *Hats.* No. Just forget about hats. If you're not in a rap band, don't wear a skull cap, either. (Hopefully by the time you read this, this style will be over.) The only time you should wear a hat is if you're going: Hunting, hiking, beaching.

- *Wallets.* You need a nice, leather one that doesn't close with Velcro. It should also be free of thousands of little useless papers and your CPR card that ran out two years ago. No man bags or messenger bags unless you are traveling or going to school!

- *Eyeglasses.* No aviator-style glasses. If you can swing it, get some contacts. If you have to wear glasses, or prefer to, go shopping and see what's in style. It won't kill you to buy a new stylish pair. Nothing says smart man quite like a smart pair of glasses. (Yes, just like men love women with glasses, women love men with glasses. Correction: Men with stylish glasses.)

- *Watches.* A watch is for telling time. Any other device on a watch besides telling time makes one look like a dork. Any nice watch with a leather band will do. (A tank watch is always good.)

- *Shoes.* Let's stop for a minute and talk about shoes. I don't think you can begin to understand how important shoes are to women. Again, women are in debt because of shoes. Do you know that many women have been known to pay as much as five-hundred—and up!—bucks for a single pair of shoes? Yeah, it's true. One of the first things the ladies will look at is your shoes. I don't know why this is, but you can tell so much about a person by just looking at their shoes. You need good shoes. Bypass Foot Locker and go to a men's shoe store. Look over what they have. If any of these shoes have a tassel, bypass them as well. Still not sure which ones to get? A good indicator is if you think a TV preacher—or a salesman—might wear them. If so, bye-bye. Good shoes have a slightly thicker sole and they are also made of leather—*real* leather. They can be in brown or black. (Unless you're a pimp, never buy a pair of shoes in any other color.) You don't have to buy five or six pairs, just one good pair to keep for your dates. Always shine your shoes. Buy a shoe-shining kit if you have to.

If you still need help, look around at a few men who have some style and check out their shoes. If you're still in doubt, ask the salesman to help you. Buying a nice pair of leather shoes in a classic style is the best way to go. (These kinds of shoes usually do not have hiking boot bottoms, nor are they hiking boots. Sorry.) You can wear these shoes with jeans or khakis or dress slacks.

The point of all this is that you want to make a good first impression. Chicks will judge you on your appearance. It may not be right and it may not be fair, but that's life. You want them to notice *you,* not your clothes.

You want to look hip and stylish but never—never!—sleazy. No gold chains, pinky rings—unless you are wearing a suit. And, if you're not in a rock band, no earrings! Yup, you heard me right. Get rid of it now. (If you have a nose ring or any other kind of ring somewhere on your body, I am assuming you work in a tattoo parlor.)

You say, *All this sounds good but I have no idea where to start.* If so, study the good men's magazines (not *Juggs*) and see what's in style. Tear a few of those pics out and take them with you when you go to shop. Also, try everything on! Bend down and over and hug yourself to make sure the seams don't creak. Check out the sleeves. They should cover your wrists when you hold your arm out straight—think about reaching for the biscuits. If you reach and your sleeve comes up over your wrist a little too far, it's too small.

Check out the hemline on your pants as well. It should drape around the top of your shoes but never above your ankle. You want clothing to fit but never skin tight. A little looser is better than a little tighter, unless, of course, you're a stripper and if you are, I shouldn't have to tell you anything about picking up chicks.

Buy the stuff *as you can afford it.* Of course, you are going to going to have to spend some money, tightwad. If you're strapped for cash, set a few bucks back every week until you have enough for one good outfit, from head to toe. Then, save some more and buy another and another. Soon, your closet will have admiring glances from all the ladies who are about to enter your life. Just don't be afraid to change your wardrobe. Be a sharp dressed man. Looking good and having good clothing is so going to boost your confidence level. And that's what we're after here. Once you have confidence, you can conquer the world.

What we learned:

- The way a man dresses is very important to a woman. She will pick out a sharp dressed man in a crowd but not the loser in Sebago's.
- Anything that is suspect in your closet needs to be thrown out. See list.
- Buy new, stylish clothes that make you look like somebody. See list.
- Don't be afraid to spend a little money.
- If you can't afford new clothes, start a clothing fund today.

Grooming.

How you groom yourself leads one to believe that you care about the way you look. In turn, this makes others care about getting to know you better.

How's your hair doing? Is it funny looking? Weird? Chopped up? Cut up? Is some of it missing? If you don't have a good haircut, it's time, my friend, to get that head of yours in as good as shape as your body and wardrobe. (You *better* be working on that, too.)

Stop going to the barbershop. Old men don't care how you look, they're just thinking about how they're gonna spend that seven bucks you're gonna give them for making a mess of your hair. If you've still got some hair on your head, get yourself an appointment with a stylist that can do something with your mop. Oh, no, you might have to spend, like, thirty bucks to do this. Don't shudder! You can forgo a DVD or wrestling pay-per-view here or there.

If you're losing your hair, you might want to consider shaving it all off and going bald. Nothing says loser quite like a comb-over—forget hair pieces, too, because any woman with a brain can detect one! Bald heads these days seem to be chick magnets. (Girls *love* to rub bald heads for some reason.) Remember, it's not the hair that attracts women, it's the confidence.

Now let's take a look at your face. First off, the unibrow. Unless you belong to a popular British band, it ain't gonna work for you. Maybe not even then. Anyway, while you're getting your hair cut, ask the stylist to wax—not shave!—

your unibrow. It's *not* an unmanly thing to do. (Very important note: If your stylish wants to "shape" your eyebrows, tell them no. Men that shape their eyebrows look weird, so don't do it. Pluck a few strays here and there, but that's all! Nothing more! Besides the unibrow, of course. You can get rid of all of it.)

Now let's move on to shaving. You guys should *always* shave your faces if you plan on doing any kissing. Women do not like to be rubbed raw by a five o'clock shadow. Let me tell you how it feels. Go grab a piece of sandpaper. Rub it as hard as you can across your forehead. Ouch!

Do you have a beard? *Why do you have a beard?* You're not ashamed of your face, are you? You might not give a damn if anyone sees it, but she kinda needs to. I bet you got a nice face under there. Let's have a look.

If you have a moustache, you need to realize that they are out of fashion and every woman in the world is praying they never come back. That's not to say they won't be back in a few millennia's, but hey, if you're willing to wait it out, that's your business.

I'm not even going to say a word about soul patches and Elvis-sized sideburns. I shouldn't have to.

And now onto your body hair. More specifically, your pubic hair. I'm willing to bet that's it's like a jungle down there. I'm not saying to completely shave it, that's just plain weird, but at least make your Johnson presentable so if she's looking for it, she don't have to ask, "Is that it, there?" (No small penis jokes here, fellas. That is not what this is about, gutter-brain.) It's easy to get it under control. Just trim and shave and use shaving gel. You should shave every day or every other day to keep it under control. Remember, it's all about presentation.

Now, on the other hand, don't go crazy and shave everything. You're not one of those guys that shaves all of his body hair, are you? Are you a swimmer or a cyclist, perhaps? If not, why are you doing it? If you have tons of hair you want to get rid of, have it waxed, otherwise, tomorrow it's going to grow right back. If you're not covered in fur, then just trim it a little.

Let's turn our focus to cologne. All you need is a touch of this stuff. If you wear too much, she'll *really* get a headache. So, put a little dab on your hands, rub your hands together, and lightly slap it on. Never, ever overpower anyone with your cologne.

You might be thinking, this is kinda of like a make-over. So what? You apparently didn't have much luck dressing like a dork and looking like a doughboy. It's time to take charge of your life and make yourself presentable to the opposite sex. The more attention you pay to yourself, the more confident you will be. And, as I have been saying, confidence is what we're after here, in case you haven't been paying attention. And, no, I'm not trying to turn you into a metrosexual.

What we learned:
- Keep yourself properly groomed.
- Get a good haircut.
- Trim pubes.

Get a good job if you don't already have one.

Let's face it. You need a better paying gig. It's time to move up. Having a good job makes anyone more confident. And knowing you can afford to date is a good feeling.

If you can get your cheap boss to give you a raise, you are tha' man! If you're like the rest of us, you can't. So why not ask another boss for a better paying job—at a different company. All you have to do is think about how you got the job you have now and do the same thing. But with a better paying job. I shouldn't have to say this, but make sure you have a job in place before you quit your current one.

During times of recession, it's best not to leave your job. But when the economy is good, go for it. However, always keep an eye out for a better paying job with more perks, even in recessions. Hey, you went to college for something, didn't you?

You don't have to be rich, but you shouldn't have to count out change for her meal at McDonald's. Women love to be pampered and you need to get used to that idea. Most women do expect to work after they marry—and have kids—but they need to know you can take care of them and their offspring if they decide they no longer want to. I know we're getting ahead of ourselves here, but I am cluing you into the way a woman's mind works. If she sizes you up and thinks you can't afford anything, she's going to turn you down. It's harsh, I know.

So get yourself a better paying job if at all possible. Failing that, you can always sell your sperm for some extra cash.

What we learned:
- It is a good idea to get a better paying gig when you can instead of always settling.
- Only quit your current job once you have a better one in place.

Your pad.

Where you live is very important if you're trying to impress a girl. Living by yourself is *more* important. If you still live at home…well, we've discussed this already.

Now let's take a look at your pad. Oh, boy, this is going to be hard. For some reason—and I think it's because mom always picked up after her boy—men don't get cleaning. Not only that, they don't understand why women don't like dirty apartments. "It's not *that* bad," you say.

Look around your pad. It *is* that bad, isn't it? If you live in a rathole, move out of it. If you have a good job and can afford it, do yourself a favor and buy a nice house or condo in a good neighborhood. This will show her you're already settled to a certain extent and won't run away when she starts to get cozy. It's also a very good investment.

If you have a roommate, how do you expect a woman to want to get busy at your place? Women need to know no one is listening—or, perhaps, watching—when they finally give it up. They are giving you something they believe is very special and they don't want an audience. (Also, they don't want you to film them in secret or otherwise. You can film yourselves having sex when you get bored with sex with each other.)

But I don't have the cash, you whine. Tough. You ain't gettin' any. Face it. Face it now. Do you want some? Then proceed.

If you already have your own pad that looks—and smells—okay, then I can just bet it's filthy. Guess what? You are going to have to do something with that pigsty you call a home. I know no one ever comes over to visit you, but that's all about to change. One of the worst things you can do is ask a chick over and allow her to see your crappy pad. If you're a slob, she probably won't want anything to do with you. Why? Because if you stay together and maybe get married—oooooooh, scary!—she's the one who will pick up after you for the rest of her life. You're showing her how you *actually* are here. And if you're a big, nasty slob, you're showing her the door.

If you can't torch the place and start over, you are going to have to clean like crazy and do a little shopping. If   you can afford it, hire a maid to swing by once a week. If not, start with the small things. The dirty dishes, for instance. Make it a habit to always clean up after yourself. Everything should be sparkling clean and all that clutter sitting around should be disposed of. If you and your new girl move in together, it's going to go in the trash anyway. Why not take care of that chore now so you'll have plenty of time to get busy?

Think clean, uncluttered and nice. If you can afford a new couch, buy one with some style and get rid of that ugly one your granny gave you to get it out of her house. And don't forget to dust your big screen TV.

A list of things that is very important:

- Clean bed sheets! If you can afford it, the higher the thread-count the better. 300-plus is always good but if you go higher, she will never want to get out of bed. (A note on silk or satin sheets— don't. You will slide right off them. Cotton is always best.)
- Toilet paper in the bathroom! Also, a good, clean toilet. Clean, clean, clean! A good, clean bathtub

in case you get into the shower together. Also, good, clean towels so you can dry her off afterwards. It wouldn't hurt to replace that bathmat, either. You do have a bathmat, don't you?

- Everything in the kitchen should be clean and rodent/pest free. Please, if you have cockroaches, get the problem taken care of.
- A nice bottle of champagne in the fridge. Don't open it unless she comes over. Maybe have a few nice snacks on hand, too. (And I don't mean Cheese Whiz.)
- How about buying some special blend coffee? I think you should.
- A nice set of silverware. (No plastic spoons!)
- A nice set of dishes and good, thick glasses that are not plastic.
- Condoms! If you have an old pack lying around, throw them out and buy new ones. (Yes, they do have expiration dates.)

Get it done and get on with your life. You don't want to spend too much time on this. Take one day a week to do all the necessary cleaning and the rest of the week, practice your new dating skills.

What we learned:
- No woman wants to visit a man who lives in a pigsty.
- Clean your pad.
- Always have toilet paper on hand.

Before you venture out...

Okay, so you're ready now, aren't you? You've got that gut under control and you've got that mop on your head trimmed up nicely and, hey, look at you! You're all spiffy in your nice, new clothes. And what's that? Mmm...you smell *so* good. Just a touch of cologne on that clean-shaven face. You look and smell good enough to eat. And if you really do in reality, some other chick will notice, too.

Before you step out that door and venture into the big, scary world of trying to pick up a beautiful girl, it's a good idea check yourself. This is to ensure that your appearance is as good as it can be. You don't want to make a bad first impression because you didn't take time to brush your teeth.

Before you go out, be sure to:
- Shower.
- Shave or trim facial hair.
- Shave and trim pubic hair. (You never know, you might get lucky!)
- Floss and brush your teeth and use mouthwash. Don't forget to gargle.
- Check for any stray hairs in nose or ears.
- Iron clothes.
- Shine shoes.
- Trim and file nails, fingers *and* toes. (Again, you never know, you might get lucky and you don't want to gouge her with your sharp toenails, do you?)

- If you're a smoker, keep a pack of spearmint gum in your pocket and pop it in before you meet others. But be sure to take it out of your mouth *after* you enter the club or wherever you're going.

If you look your best, chicks will see you at your best. They will see *you* and chances are they will like what they see. And that's the impression you want. Don't sabotage yourself before you even get to the date by not taking time to look your best. *Take time to do this.* It shows the ladies that you care about yourself and that will make them want to care about getting to know you better. This stuff will become a habit and soon, you won't want to leave your place without looking your best.

What we learned:
- Always groom yourself properly before you hit the door.
- Look in the mirror and make sure everything looks okay.

Good taste.

It's good to know that women like men with good taste, whether it's in cars, wine or clothing. Again, it's the James Bond thing. He has it going on. He knows how to work these chicks like nobody's business. Of course, he's a fictitious character but you can still learn a thing or two from him.

Shocking to know, but it is possible to be interested in more than the sports page or the big game. You can cultivate good taste by reading, watching other people, traveling, surfing the internet, watching good documentaries, and studying different cultures. (If you watch documentaries, you'll always have something to talk about on dates.) Take a stroll in a museum every once in a while. Open a book and the world opens up to you. Don't just read comic books, read Bukowski, Fitzgerald, Keroauc and, of course, the other basic classics. You'll be surprised how good they are. Watch classic movies like *Alfie* and *La Dolce Vita*. Cultivate a thirst for knowledge on all subjects. Don't just see the world around you, see the world outside of the one you live. Another way to put this: Think outside the box.

Another thing to notice about Mr. Bond is this: He loves women. You have to love women in order to be good with them. Think about the old masters: Dean Martin, Sinatra, Elvis. They all have something in common and it's simple. They loved women, each and every one of them. They didn't discriminate. They loved all women of all shapes and sizes. If you love women, half the work is already done. And by love

I mean, you think they're great, that there's nothing better than a woman. All of them fascinate you. They make you smile. If you're a misogynous bastard—which means you hate women—no amount of work is going to help you. And if you do, you need some help.

What we learned:
- Women love men with good taste. Cultivate it.
- Think outside the box.
- Don't be a misogynous bastard.

Be a man!

Just a quick note on this. If any sort of confrontation happens where the woman you're with is in some sort of trouble, be a man and defend her honor. Stick up for her even if it's just telling some jerk to step back. You will find that the more beautiful your honey is, the more likely she is gonna get hit on. You don't want some jerk taking your place before you even get started.

One thing to remember, though, is that if the guy is bigger than you, just try to solve the problem by having a little talk. If you do get into a fight and he beats the crap out of you, don't say I didn't warn you. And don't ever pick fights to show her how strong you are. Just show her when and if the time comes.

Added bonus: It is a huge aphrodisiac for women to see their man stick up for them. She will be all over you once it's over. *He can protect me! He stood up for me! I love him soooo much! He is so getting laid tonight!*

Think I'm lying? Oh, boy, you don't know squat then.

What we learned:
- Be the man and you might just get yourself a sex kitten.
- Try to work out any problems with talk first.

Bitchy-beautiful girls.

Don't you just love 'em? They got it goin' on! They are the best. They know how to dress that tight little body of theirs to make your jaw drop. They also know how to crush you like a bug. So, this begs the question: Are all beautiful women bitches? As always, it depends on the girl. And it depends on her circumstances. A girl can be bitchy-beautiful because some jerk hurt her once. A girl can be bitchy-beautiful because her daddy gave her everything and told her she was a princess. Regardless, now the rest of the world has to suffer.

Having said that, let me say this: Never, *ever* let a woman demean you. I don't care how pretty she is, she's not worth it. Once you do, she's got your balls and you really need them for yourself. Stand up to chicks like this. Remember that no chick wants a wimp and if she's testing you and you fail, she will consider you a wimp. Who wants to be a wimp?

How will you know if she's testing you? She may do odd things like ask you to dance with a gay guy or give her a lap dance or ask you to take your shirt off at a club. Anything that is a little weird or unmanly, don't do. Remember, she's just testing you to see if she can push you around. Don't let her!

Another word on beautiful but not necessarily bitchy girls: Just because she looks like she is out of your league doesn't necessarily mean she is. She could have been raised in a trailer and have no self confidence. She could be waiting on someone to talk to *her.* I know that a lot of guys are interested in me, but for some reason, they won't make a move. Why? They think I'll turn them down. If you like her, why not give it a try? All she can do is say no and you won't have to spend the rest of your life asking yourself, "Why didn't I ask her out?" She might say yes. But then again, she might say no. However, with all the confidence you've acquired thus far, your fear of getting turned down should start diminishing.

What we learned:
- Bitchy, beautiful girls can be a pain in the butt. Make sure she's worth it.
- Just because she's beautiful doesn't mean she gets hit on a lot. Why not try? All she can do is say no. If she does, move on and don't let it bother you at all.

A word on aggressive girls.

Yes, they are out there. They do exist. There are girls who come on strong, hit hard and then hit the door. We will kindly refer to them as the *aggressive girls*.

Some men can handle the aggressive girl and some can't. If you decide you'd like to get to know her better, hang on. It's going to be a bumpy ride.

If you're lucky enough to hook up with an aggressive girl, all you need to know is that she will make the first move and she will be in totally in control. All you have to do is wait. Hopefully, you won't get hurt. Just watch yourself, though. Aggressive girls tend to drink a lot. And, yeah, they can drink you under the table. Keep an eye on how much *you're* drinking so you don't miss out on your opportunity to have a wild, crazy night. But don't expect to see her in the morning.

Should you hook up with one of them, pat yourself on the back. She will more than likely take care of everything and if she doesn't like you, she'll let you know and not waste your time. But don't think that because she's coming on strong that she's a ho-bag. This means, if she'd coming on strong, she might just be playing you. Which means, you might get lucky and you might not. It all depends on her mood at the time. That's just her personality shining through. Not all people are meek and mild. Thank God.

How to spot an aggressive girl? Look for her to be dancing on the tables. She'll be the loud one having the most fun at any party. Amble on up to her and let the rest take care if itself. (Also note that if she's aggressive in the club or bar, she'll be aggressive in the sack. If this intimidates you in the least, keep your distance. She won't let you say no.)

What we learned:
- Aggressive girls can be fun.
- Maybe you'll get lucky enough and come across one.

Do not disrespect her.

Before you do anything, take a look at yourself and stop blaming everyone else for your shortcomings. And don't blame her if she turns you down.

Don't make assumptions about her being:
- A slut.
- A whore.
- Any other bad word you can think of to cover your own inadequacies.
- A homemaker.
- A home wrecker.
- A bitch.

Please, before you go out, remember that. Don't do anything that will make her hate your guts. I am more than sure you are a nice guy. Act like one.

Someone once told me they ask every girl out they see. Why? I don't know, either, but I guess the dude thought the law of averages was on his side. The more he asked out, the more likely he was going to hook up. The only problem is that he looks a little too desperate. Never show desperation. Don't be stupid. Don't act stupid. If she doesn't want you, let it be and be gracious.

Before we move on, let's talk abut the basic rules of attracting women.

The basic rules of attracting women:

- *Let her come to you.* That's right, let her come to you. You can give her the "eye", maybe a smile or even send her a drink. But if she doesn't give you the signal to approach, leave her alone. If, however she does give you the signal, then it's all up to you. If you don't take the hint that's it's okay to move in, she won't come to you. You've just missed an opportunity to get to know her.
- Women are in control. You are not and you never will be. You can whine, "But I saw this guy in a bar approaching women and getting hit on left and right." Some men just know how to play it better. If you watched closely, he lets the women do all the touchy-feely at first. Later on, he can get touchy-feely when she invites him back to her crib. Never do the touchy-feely with a woman you've just met. Let *her* do it.
- Women like men who are comfortable with themselves.
- Women want men who are both physically and emotionally strong. The stronger you are, the stronger her babies will be. That's the reason. It's true. It's all about Natural Selection. She probably doesn't even realize this, but it's a basic biological fact.
- Be the guy who is willing to rise to the challenge to be a better mate, a better partner.
- Women like men who are good listeners and who ask questions about them.

The pick-up artist.

I shouldn't have to say this, but I am going to. If you think you have a great pick-up line, keep it to yourself. Pick-up lines never, ever work on chicks. You will get a "Loser!" or an eye roll whenever you attempt one.

But how *do* you approach her? How do you know *when* to approach her? Watch for the signals.

Signals:
- A smile thrown in your direction.
- A coy look.
- She runs her hands through her hair.
- She's staring at you and when you look at her, she looks away almost in embarrassment, like you caught her staring. (Which, of course, you *did*.)
- She sends you a drink.
- She bites her lips or licks her lips.
- She jerks her head for you to come over.

Now that you have the signal, it's time to move in. As you approach her, remember, she's just as nervous as you are, if not more so. Put her at ease by being a gentleman and by giving her a nice smile.

What women think when they first zone in on a guy:
- "He better do something to impress me."
- "He looks okay, though."
- "I want to turn him down."

- "I wish he'd do something to let me know he likes me."
- "God, I hope I don't make a fool of myself."
- "I feel very shy and nervous all of a sudden."
- "Oh, no, here he comes. What can I do? Act like I don't care. Yeah, that's good."
- "Oh, damn it, I just giggled."
- "If he comes on too strong, I am going to slap him."
- "Why does he keep looking over here and not doing anything?"
- "Well, if he's coming over, I wish he'd hurry. I don't have all night!"
- "I hope he's nice and doesn't use any pick-up lines."
- "Oh, God! Here he comes! Be calm, be calm!"
- "Yeah, he looks nice. Good shoes! If he asks for my number, I will probably give it to him."

She wants you to impress her. But, she doesn't want you to overpower her, not just yet. Keep in mind that you're starting off as friends. Oh, no, the dreaded friend zone! *Yes.* If you think like this and get your dirty little mind off sex, then your chances of scoring are increased. Why? She automatically thinks that you want to have sex and she's not easy. If you put *her* in the friend zone first, she'll be dying to get out of it. So, therefore, put her in the friend zone and more than likely, you will find yourself out of it.

Trade secret: She wants to be unimpressed. She wants to turn you down. She doesn't want to be bothered by anyone. But then, she wants you to be the aggressor. She wants you to make the first move. But if you make a move too soon, she might think you're a creep. Damned if you do and damned if you don't.

My advice? Beat her at her game. God only knows when the "right" time to do something is. If and when you get that signal, summon your balls and approach her. If you've misread the signals and she ignores you, just say, "Well, nice talking to you," and walk away. Always be a gentleman. More than likely, this will make her feel bad for being a bitch.

When you walk over to her, say:
- "Hi, how's it going?"
- "Hey, I'm Bob and you are?"

Asking her name is important because it forces her to tell you who she is and opens the conversation. Never act stupid, even if you are. Sure, you will be nervous and maybe stumble over your words, but never do anything stupid like give her a lame pickup line or reach out and grab her booby. Women are taught by their parents and everyone else to see through that. It's not funny, it's not cute. Go up and say, "Hi" and let her talk to you. The rest, if you act cool, is going to take care of itself.

The point is to improvise in conversation. Just let whatever happens happen. Don't put too much time or thought into what you're going to say as it will come off as staged. Keep in mind that she's a normal person and talking to her shouldn't be any different than talking to any other person you don't already know.

Remember if she rejects you, she might just be:
- Involved in a relationship already.
- Married with kids.
- A lesbian.
- Heartbroken over some other guy.
- Just plain mean and miserable.

Rejection doesn't always have to do with you, you know? There are extenuating circumstances. She might like you but because she's got some baggage, she can't go out with you.

It's also good to keep in mind that this woman isn't necessarily going to change your world. She might be shallow. She might steal your stereo. She might not be worth it once you've gotten to know her. But you need to try. And you're going to. Expend some effort and you should get something in return. Expend nothing and get nothing.

Wait a minute. Before you approach her—or any other woman for that matter—make sure she isn't already taken. If you have no way of finding out, look for a ring of some sort. A big diamond is a good indicator some other guy already has his hooks in her. Also, a wedding ring should speak volumes. If you have no way of telling, go ahead and talk to her, then slip it in, easy-like, "You don't have a boyfriend, do you?"

There you go. You will find out and you can move on with your life. And if she does have a boyfriend and is thinking about dumping him, you can move in and snatch her right up.

Warning: *Said boyfriend might be a jealous freak who might come after you. Make sure she's worth it!*

What we learned:
- Before you approach any woman, make sure she's available.
- Women are just as nervous as you are when they meet someone new.
- Never use lame pick-up lines.
- Rejection isn't always about you.

I've got a crush on you.

Maybe you don't want a stable of beautiful women. Maybe you have your eye on someone in particular. She works where you do or she's the clerk at the video store or she's a stripper at your local club. Wherever she is, you want her and you want her bad. She's gorgeous. She has the perfect body and...

Anyway. Take a good look at the woman of your dreams. You're thinking that you don't have a chance in hell with her and that you might as well throw in the towel and give this one up. She might not be interested in a guy like you. She *might* be out of your league.

You know what? She might not be.

If you've been reading this book so far and have followed my advice, it shouldn't shock you to know you've got a good chance with this chick. And why shouldn't you? You're in good shape, you dress well, you have good manners and you are prepared to kick some guy's butt if he messes with her.

Get yourself ready and out that door. You are going to ask this chick out on a date and see once and for all if she will have anything to do with you. Then, if she turns you down, you can move on with your life and onto all the other hot chicks that are waiting on you as we speak.

Before you ask her out, why not start a dialogue with her? Whenever you see her, smile and say hello. Doing this a few times allows you to develop rapport. As long as you approach her with a smile, she should smile in return. She's going to know what's up, believe me.

If she returns your smile and engages in your conversations, something about you impresses her. And how will you know?

Look for signs:
- Have you caught her staring at you, then looking away quickly?
- Has she given you a shy, small smile?
- Has she ever tapped you on the shoulder or touched your arm?
- Has she ever told you a joke?
- Has she done anything to indicate there's an interest?

If you're getting these signs, go ahead and ask her out.

Here's a few examples of what to say:
- "Hey, do you want to get a bite to eat after work?"
- "I was thinking that we could go out sometime, if you like."
- "Have you heard about the concert series in the park? Would you like to go with me?"
- "How about a cup of coffee?"

Ask her, set the date—like, "How about next week, on Wednesday around seven?"—and be on your way. Also, you want her to know you're interested, but at the same time, don't come on too strong. Wait and listen to what she's saying.

It is important to note that you should apply these same rules to any situation. It's always "Proceed with caution" with any woman because you never know how they'll react. Look for signs. If she's smiling and being friendly that's always a good indicator she likes you. If, however, she runs away and avoids you, it's not.

Another word on women you work with. This is definitely "proceed with caution" because of all that sexual harassment stuff. Just chat with her and maybe tell her you and some other work buddies are going to bar after work. Then ask if she'd like to join you. If she says no, then no big deal. But be very careful. If you start to date her and then break up, it's going to get hairy. Be prepared to feel awkward.

The point is to get it done and get on with your life. If she says no, there are better women out there for you. Move on. Don't fixate on it. Be gracious in defeat. Remember: Each woman is totally different. Once you've got one figured out, another one will throw you a curve ball.

So did you ask her out? Did she turn you down? Well, so what? You gave it a try. I'm betting even if she did turn you down, she's thinking of you and you might just get lucky enough and she'll ask you out in a few weeks. This is why it's so important to handle rejection graciously. If you get too upset, she's going to think you're weird and be glad she turned you down. But if you take it in stride, she's going to want to know what's up with you.

What we learned:
- The woman you have a crush on may like you.
- Start a dialogue with her by saying "hi" when you see her.
- Always smile and act friendly.
- Be confident in your approach when you ask her out. (Already have a plan of what you want to do—dinner and a movie, etc.)
- If she turns you down, move on. Never be a sore loser!

How to talk to a woman.

After you've got the "signal", which we talked about earlier, it's time to walk right up to this girl and get things going. It is so important to know how to start that initial conversation. Without the conversation, there can be no "getting to know you" date. And we all know that there is no simple way to ask a woman out. There is no magical potion to take to make it any easier. The thing is, she's either going to say yes or she's going to say no.

You may not believe this, but when women are asked what really works when a man is trying to pick them up, most will say, "He smiled at me." Never underestimate the power of a smile! Of course, a lecherous grin isn't going to cut it. A smile should work wonders with anyone. A smile disarms even the biggest bitch on the planet. That's why earlier in the book I said that it is important for your choppers to look their best.

So how do you do it? How do you start that initial conversation? Simple. Walk up to her, smile and say, "Hi." Wait for her to respond and after she does, introduce yourself. And then…*Get her to talk about herself.* If you can get her talking about herself, all you're going to have to do is nod every so often. Asking questions about her work or where she went to school or whatever is a good way to get her talking. Women love to talk and when it's about them, be prepared to be there all night.

When talking, you should:
- Never contradict her.
- Never roll your eyes.
- Never touch her unless she's touched you first! Not even to get an eyelash off her face. Just tell her she's got one and if she leans in for you to get it, get it. But not unless invited!
- Remember her name and put it into the conversation, "So, Jane, how long have you lived here?"
- Never stare at other chicks while talking to her.
- Never look distracted.

It is important to understand that once you have her talking, you have an opportunity to date her. Don't blow it. Use the guidelines for talking from the examples I've provided. This should work every time. If it doesn't, you're doing something wrong or you're trying too hard. Don't try too hard! Don't act desperate! Don't give her a reason to say no.

A few icebreakers:
- "Do you have the time?" (If you have a watch on, don't use this one, unless it's broken.)
- Compliment her on something, like her watch or earrings.
- "Hi, how are you?"

Asking any open-ended question will spur her attention. This will get her talking and the rest should take care of itself. There is no science or mystery to it. It's all about making a little connection with someone for a period of time. Doing it this way ensures that you won't have much embarrassment and she won't call you a loser. If she does, she's a royal bitch and you're better off without her.

Remember that if she's not talking much or looking around anxiously this doesn't mean she doesn't want to talk. She could be very nervous. *She* could be shy. Watch for the signs. See if she's interested in you. If she is, she'll let you know.

After you've talked for a while, decide if you want to get her phone number. If you do…

Say this:
- "I really have to get going, but I'd love to talk to you some more. Can I get your number? Maybe we could go out sometime."

When you ask for it, ask for it with confidence, as if you don't expect her to turn you down. Also, don't stumble over your words so you'll have to repeat yourself. The thing is, it's not that hard to talk to a woman. And talk to her as if you're just shooting the breeze. Never let her in on the fact that you're *that* interested. But, of course, if you're talking to her, she probably already knows you're interested.

A few more guidelines:
- Never try to outsmart a woman.
- Never smother her.
- Never touch her unless invited.
- Never use lame pick-up lines.
- Never disrespect her.
- Never approach a woman who's wearing a scowl.

Some places you can pick her up:
- Parties.
- Bars.
- Clubs.
- Restaurants.
- Grocery stores.
- Video stores.
- Bookstores.
- The post office.
- The train station.
- Just about anywhere in public.

You always need some of your buddies to go with you when you're out at clubs or parties. Never stand alone by yourself. This looks creepy and you'll be known as that guy "alone in the corner drinking himself into oblivion." Never, ever drink too much. Keep yourself in check as no chick likes a horny, drunken fool.

What we learned:
- Approach a woman with a smile and a "Hi."
- Introduce yourself.
- Get her to talk about herself.
- Ask open-ended questions.

Rehearsal for talking to chicks.

Let's get right to the point and the point of this chapter is rehearsing for talking to chicks. It is comprised of pretend dialogue. You don't have to use it verbatim or even use it; this is just to let you know how it usually goes. It might also be a good idea to practice with yourself—or a friend—in front of a mirror. Don't feel like a fool. Make the mistakes before you go out. The key is to be prepared. The more you do this, the better you will get at it and soon it will be second nature. That's your goal. Expect to strike out a few times before you get a hit.

Also, you don't have to create a script to follow. If she says something you didn't expect and you don't have an answer, you'll end up getting tongue-tied. Be willing to be flexible.

And, as always, before you approach her, make a little eye contact. Meet her eyes a few times before you proceed. If she's not meeting your gaze at all, proceed with caution or don't proceed at all. Remember to wait for the signal to step to it. And if you're getting it, you'll know it.

What are the signals?
- She will throw you a smile.
- She will give you a shy or coy look.
- She will look a little nervous, as if you caught her staring at you.

The key is to *not* stare at her. Casually glance over. Watch her for a few moments and try to catch her gaze. Once you do, give her a smile, wait a few seconds for her to respond and then immediately look away and start talking with one of your friends. This is what I like to call the "whatever" approach. Whatever happens is fine. If she likes you, whatever. If she doesn't, whatever. You're just there to be sociable, just like her. Remember it's all in the attitude. You're just a friendly, good natured guy. But you're also confident enough to know that you have the ability to talk to a woman.

Okay. Let's say you're sitting at the bar and a hot chick sits down near you. Wait a few minutes and then glance in her direction and say—loudly enough for her to hear you— "Hi."

"Hi," she says.

"I know this is stupid," you say. "But I heard this really great pick-up line the other day. Wanna hear it?"

Screech! You say, *But you told me not to ever use pick-up lines!* Okay, you're not using a pick-up line here to actually pick her up. You're using a pick-up line to start a conversation. Doing it this way will disarm her. Try it and see. This is more like a joke than a pick-up line, okay? (Also, if you can't handle doing it as a joke, don't use it. Just ask if she'd like a drink or something.)

"Sure," she says.

"I'm one and you're one, let's get together and make two," you say and laugh. "How bad is that?"

"It's terrible," she says and laughs.

"I know," you say. "I didn't offend you, did I?"

"No, I'm a big girl," she says. "I can take it."

"So," you say. "Tell me a little about yourself. Where do you work?"

This gets her to talking about herself. Once you do this, it's in her court. Just continue to interject other little questions as she's yakking. This is really the key to talking to women. They love to yammer about themselves.

Questions like:
- Where do you work?
- Do you enjoy your job?
- Where did you go to school?
- What was your major?
- Did you see that movie?

After she's talked for a while, tell her you have to get going, but you'd love to continue the conversation, maybe over dinner sometime. And ask for her number. And you're done. Remember, you should exude confidence at all times, even if she rejects you. Take it like a man and say, "Oh, that's cool." She will want to know what's up with you.

But if she's interested in you, she will want to go out on a date. And if she's not interested, then you're back in the game again. Repeat this and surely to God you will eventually have success of some kind. The important thing to keep in mind is that the first few times you do this, expect to strike out. You're honing your craft and it will take several attempts to get it right. Don't be afraid to make mistakes and don't be afraid to try again. Tell yourself you have to do this exercise and soon it will come as second nature.

As you do this, remember: It's okay to be a little nervous. You're human, aren't you? It's okay if you embarrass yourself a few times. Once you get over your initial hesitation, it will get easier and easier. If you do embarrass yourself, laugh it off. Women expect a little humility because it means you're not going to expect too much of them and that helps take the pressure off.

Here are a few more scenarios…

If you're at a club and she's dancing, buy her a drink, take it over to her and say, "Looks like you might be thirsty." Hand her the drink, smile and walk away. Go and sit down somewhere. If she was impressed, she will find you.

If you see the woman of your dreams at a park, whether she's walking her dog or jogging, don't approach her until she has stopped moving, then throw her a smile and a "Hello."

And wait for her to respond. Then start a conversation. Remember the most important thing to know is they have to give you the signal to approach. Once you get it, approach with confidence. But you will first have to let them know you're a little interested and you do that by: Giving her a smile or a "Hello".

If you're dining out with your buddies and see a woman you like, why not send over a dessert? Women love chocolate. After you send it, wait for her to respond. If she doesn't, you're only out a few bucks.

One last thing. Once you meet a woman, you will probably shake her hand after you've introduced yourself. Give her a nice handshake and then withdraw your hand. Never let it linger. Women hate bad handshakes. Remember, women are always tying to protect their personal space so it's best you don't get too close. You have to be invited in before you can invade it. Also, don't kiss her hand or cheek—*ick!*—or try to give her a hug. I've seen this on a lot of TV reality shows and it just looks creepy. So, it's not a good idea to do this in real life. Unless you're willing to take the chance of getting slapped.

That should give you plenty to chew on for a while. The key is always confidence. Have confidence and everything else should fall into place. Using these methods should get you in the door.

What we learned:
- Talking to a woman isn't that hard.
- Just act like she's any other normal human being.
- Don't be afraid to strike out a few times.
- Starting a conversation is the first step to picking her up.
- Always smile and act nice, but be confident.
- If she turns you down, be gracious and move on.

Kids.

There may be a possibility that the woman of your dreams has a kid or two. Though I have never understood why, this freaks some men out. At least you know she's fertile. For some reason guys think because she's got a kid or two she's damaged goods.

That is the way a jerk thinks. What should it matter? Apparently her first relationship didn't work out. This doesn't mean that if you get into a relationship with her that it's doomed from the get-go. If she has a kid—or kids—grow up! I know that a lot of guys don't want an Instant Family and that's fine. I also know a lot of super-hot chicks who have kids and don't date much because of it. (And I mean *super*-hot.)

So, just find out before you take her out if she's got any kids. If she's got a few, just smile and move away from her if it makes you that uncomfortable. But don't treat her like she's got the plague!

One more note, just because she's got kids doesn't mean she's easy. Don't ever assume she's going to have sex with you just because you bought her a meal. Always be kind and respectful. That's building good Karma and we could all use some good Karma.

What we learned:
- Some women already have kids. If you don't want to deal with that, be upfront about it. Never waste her time.

Don't try to impress her.

I can just hear you asking, *What? Don't try to impress her? What's this?!* Calm down, boy, and sit back and listen.

Yes, you're going to impress her by doing stuff like cleaning your pigsty and getting some new threads. But if *you* go out of your way to tell her how great you are, she's just going to think you're either a liar or an egomaniac. Never, ever try to convince anyone of your greatness. They will either see it or not. Never, ever be too obvious. Obvious=desperate and a chick can see right through that.

Remember, the first few dates are reserved for her. Make her feel special. Let her talk your ear off. Be considerate to her and keep your distance. If she wants you, she will let you know.

Do little things that speak for themselves:
- Open doors.
- Unlock her side of the car first.
- Pay the check.
- And all that other stuff I've told you about.

Avoid talking:
- About yourself. You're there to get to know her.
- About how great you are.
- About your conquests—real or otherwise.
- About your poetry and at all costs, please do not ever ask her to read it. You know it sucks as most poetry does.

When she says, "Tell me about yourself," tell her about yourself. Tell her where you went to school and where you live and work and all that. She's asking this so she can tell what kind of guy you are. Let her know upfront about your work and all that. Talk about yourself, but always stop every once in a while and ask her a question like, "Where did you grow up?" and stuff like that. Treat her as if she were any other "normal" person you want to get to know better.

And that's all you're doing here. Sure, you want to get laid, but this time is reserved to get to know her. Use this time to just *be*. Stop worrying about your penis for a few minutes and engage in a conversation with another human being. Stop worrying about after the date and stop thinking about what color her panties are. Don't ever expect more than what you have in the moment. If you get it, great. If not, why worry and bitch and complain about it? This is called dating, after all. This is her time and treat it as such. Being respectful is going to get you major points. Pushing yourself on her and trying to get into pants will get you the cold shoulder.

Important note: Touchy, feely, kissy is really creepy. Even if you are from a family that does this, try to control yourself. Women absolutely hate these kinds of guys. Keep your hands to yourself! She will give you the signal to touch her and it will be subtle—a nod of the head, a look into the eyes, chin in the air as she stares into your eyes. Just don't get familiar too soon.

In the same vein, desperation/egomania speaks for itself. Don't tell her how many women you've slept with in order to impress her. More than likely it will just piss her off and if she asks, just shrug and ask her the exact same question. Say that you prefer not to kiss and tell. She *will* change the subject. Neither one of you need to know that anyway because no matter how many it was, it's always *too* many. Reserve this fight for when you've been going out for a while. (And once you get to it, I feel for both of you.)

What we learned:
- Don't try to impress her by telling her how great you are. Impress her by being clean, stylish and in good shape. These things speak for themselves.
- Avoid talking—or overtalking—about yourself. Just give her a little something to go on. If she wants to know, she'll ask.
- Never brag.
- Remember, at first, this is all about her. Get to know her.

Bad signs.

Just so you will know, there are women out there who will try and take advantage of you and your good nature. Be cautious with a hot chick if she asks to borrow money, credit cards, etc. If she steals your stuff, dump her. You could ask why she did it but she's just going to act like she doesn't know what you're talking about.

There are women out there who will use you. Believe me, there are. If you're not getting anything out of it, why bother? And if you are getting something out of it and don't mind, then that is your business, mister. I'm just giving you a head's up on this one.

What we learned:
- Some chicks are out to use you.
- Be cautious if she starts asking for money, etc.

The way a woman flirts.

A woman can flirt in various ways and if you know what signs to look for, you can ascertain if she likes you or not. Wanna find out if she's really interested? Here's how. And this is universal; it has been going on forever. It won't change tomorrow.

When a woman sees a in whom she's interested:
- She will smile.
- She will lift her eyebrows.
- She will open her eyes wide to gaze at a man.
- She will tilt her head to the side.
- She will look away, almost in embarrassment.
- She might giggle nervously and hide her face in her hands.
- She will toss or play with her hair.
- She will raise her shoulders.
- She may mirror his actions, like look at her watch after he looks at his.
- And, more than likely, she will get tongue-tied. As I've said, she's just as nervous as you are. Keep that in mind and give her a break if she's acting strange.

If she does any of these things in any order or at any time, this means she's interested in you. If you don't get any of these signals, it's a sign for you to stay away!

What we learned:
- Watch for the signs to see if she digs you. If you ain't getting any, she ain't getting you.

You can't dance.

You're at a club and this really hot chick pulls you to the dance floor. Now what the hell are you supposed to do? Listen. Don't bust a groove. Let her dance around you. Don't shake your butt out there or do your famous break-dancing moves. Don't raise the roof. Don't do the cabbage patch. Just let her groove around you and keep your eyes on her. Hopefully, it will be over very soon.

A woman always leads on the dance floor—unless it's ballroom dancing—or you just end up looking like a fool. Follow her movements if she's gotten you out there. That way, you look like you're just interested in her but you don't end up looking like a dork. Don't stand still but do move a little, but not too much as you'll end up looking like you're either gay or a dancing fool.

What we learned:
- You can't dance.
- If she makes you dance, don't stand still. Just follow her movements but don't overdo it.

Make her laugh. But don't try to be funny.

Contradiction? Hardly. If you can make her laugh, she's gonna stick around a little while to see what else you can do. But *try* to make her laugh and all you're gonna hear is crickets. So, therefore, no corny jokes and if you have to say something funny and witty, save it. It will always come out wrong. Don't act too funny. Most people are not natural comedians and more than likely you aren't either.

Sucks for you, but hey, that's the way the world works. Just be yourself. If you are, that's a good impression.

Another lovely lady I know said this, "This guy, bless his heart, this guy was so un-funny it was almost funny. He told these corny jokes and whenever there was an opening for him to say something 'funny', he would. I might have given him a chance but he really got on my nerves. It was one of the longest dates I've ever been on."

Don't be this guy. You could end up in a dating book!

If you want her to laugh, why not learn a few—clean!—jokes. (Dirty jokes are a real turn-off.) Self-deprecating humor is always good, too. But be natural. If you can't tell a good joke, then don't. As your nervousness wanes, say something a little funny. But never overdo it. Never get on her nerves. Never try to make her laugh. If you do this, she will laugh at you—behind your back.

What we learned:
- Don't try too hard to make her laugh.
- A little self-deprecating humor can be good in small doses.

Women are the world's mystery.

I admit it. Women are hard to figure out. What works for one will never work with another. But we all have basic needs and desires. We all want a good man. Be a good man and you will find yourself a good woman.

Some things that women really like:
- Compliments. Compliment her dress or her jewelry or anything. She spent a long time getting ready! She'll be glad someone noticed.
- Chocolate.
- New shoes.
- A man who is good in bed.
- A man who pays for dinner.
- A man who can work on her car.
- A man who listens to her.
- Planning her dream wedding.
- Jewelry.
- Men.

You've got her number, now what?

Call her! I mean, what else are you gonna do with it? Are you gonna play the stupid waiting game? You know which one I'm talking about. It's where you get a chick's phone number and wait two, three, four days to call her. Don't! If you do this, it means that you're a game player. You asked for that number, now summon your balls and call her already! *Man,* you say, *this seems harder than getting her number in the first place.* That's because you still fear rejection. Well, you'll never know until you try and you asked for that number for a reason. For all you know, she's waiting on you to call. She wants you to call. And if she doesn't, she won't pick up.

Remember, if she didn't want you to call, she wouldn't have given you her number. If she gave you a fake number, then she's just a bitch. It's that simple.

So, wait until the next day. Maybe in the evening sometime when you know she'll answer. Say, hello, hi, this is—whatever your name is—we met at—wherever you met—and let it go from there. Don't be afraid. She's a person just like you. Sure, she's got a nice set of tits, but, hey, she's still human.

So, you've got her on the phone. Now what? Be yourself. That should be easy enough. Talk to her for a little while, asking about her day and her work and all that. Then, ask her out for a date. You should always have a plan, by the way. Whether you want to take her for a nice dinner or to a concert or wherever. *You make the plans.* Women hate it when guys don't know where to go. Never say, "We'll go where you want to." No, no, no! Say, "I thought we could try this new restaurant. How about it?" Or, "I know this nice little restaurant…"

If you call your chick and she doesn't answer, leave a very short, brief message. Say something like, "This is Bob. We met at the bookstore. Anyway, just wanted to call and see what's going on. My number is 867-5309. Thanks."

And don't hesitate. Say it like you mean it. Say it like a man. Just say it, for God's sake! And let her call you back. If she doesn't, she's not interested and you just saved yourself some embarrassment and time. Make sure you don't grovel by calling her back several times. If you think something got screwed up with the message, wait until the next day and give it another try. If you still don't hear from her, it's because she doesn't want to talk to you.

Now, if and when she returns your message, make sure she remembers you by saying something like, "Yeah, hello. I met you at the grocery store?"

She says, "Yeah, I know who you are."

And then ask her how it's going. Again—important thing here—let her talk! Ask about her day and her job and her cat. Of course, she should ask you about yourself, too, and when she does, give short, nice answers.

And blah, blah, blah.

Once you've let her talk for a few minutes, step in and ask her out. You should already know where you want to take her. Whether it's to dinner, for drinks or to see some band. Ask her, let her answer and there you go. It's done.

You're getting good at this, aren't you?

What we learned:
- Once you get her number, call her the next day.
- Be sure to ask her out on a date once you've got her on the phone.
- Have a plan of where you want to take her.

If you hound her...

You've just taken her out and had a nice time. The night is ending and you're at her front door. You spent some money and now you want something back for it. You try to push yourself on your date.

You are headed for trouble.

First of all, just because you spent a little money doesn't mean that you're going to get some. You can never make assumptions about a woman. As soon as you do, she will turn on a dime and do the exact opposite of what you think she will do. You think that if you "work" her a little, you can have sex. Or, rather, you're entitled to have sex.

Nope.

Don't "work" her to get "some"! *Ever!* If she wants to have sex with you, she will let you know. Drop all your stupid rules, like no kissing on the first date or whatever else you made up in grade school. Dumb, dumb, dumb and you're sabotaging yourself. Chicks pick up on this stuff pretty easily and know it's all a scam to make her "want" you. Most times, it just sounds corny.

If you are trying to make her a conquest, she'll find out and hate your guts for it. Don't get upset if you've worked a girl and she won't put out. Don't take it out on her by demeaning her; you're only making yourself look like an idiot. And a psycho. If you're that desperate to get laid, hire an escort and get it over.

I'm just saying that if she won't have sex with you do not *ever* try to talk her into it. Do you want to be someone's bad memory? If she doesn't really want you and she has sex with you, all you're ever going to be is a bad, bad memory. She will cringe when she thinks of you afterwards. She will shudder and want to take a bath. Do you want her to refer to you as, "That guy who almost raped me?" Think about that before you let your hormones get the best of you.

What we learned:

- Never assume a woman is going to give it up just because you bought her dinner.
- Don't "work" her in order to get some.

Are you stalker material? Don't be!

Have you met the girl of your dreams and she turned you down? Now you can't get her out your head, can you? You turned into a stalker and...well, stalked her.

First of all, this is illegal and extremely creepy. This is the kind of stuff that will mess your life up for good.

If you find that you:
- Stand outside her apartment.
- Wait outside her work.
- Call her and then hang up.
- "Find" yourself being in the same place as her a lot.

Then you are stalker material. Don't be! Stop this behavior right now. If she doesn't like you, there's nothing you can do about it. She isn't going to come around. Leave her alone. Go find another chick to love on.

If you find yourself obsessing about one particular girl, find a way to get her out of your system. Maybe she's a girl that you've had a crush on and never had the courage to talk to. Maybe you had one date or shared a drink but she doesn't want anything to do with you now. *Take the hint!* Get lost. Find a new girl and see if she works out or, failing that, find a new hobby or work on your poetry. Anything you can do to get her out of your mind, do it.

You howl, *But it was meant to be!* No it wasn't! She doesn't want you, so forget her! Don't let this obsessive train of thoughts get you into some major trouble. This chick could have a mean older brother or an ex-boyfriend who's a wrestler. She could have your butt kicked three ways to Sunday. She could also have you arrested.

A good friend of mine told me this story, "I went on one date with this guy. One date and he kept calling me and then I saw him outside my work one day. It creeped me out, but not as much as it angered me. He would email me these long pathetic letters that just made me cringe, as if that would change my mind or something. I mean, I didn't like him, okay? Sorry! Please leave me alone, creep! Finally, I just confronted him and told him to leave me the hell alone. He finally did after that. Thank God. I thought I was going to have to get a restraining order or something."

You don't want to be Mr. Creepy. *Ever.* Move on and away from this chick or you are asking to be sent to jail.

What we learned:
- If you stalk her, you just might go to jail and become someone's bitch.

Is she stalker material?

Yes, as unlikely as it may seem, there are women out there who might become obsessed with you. You may find that she's showing up at your work or leaving weird messages on your machine. If so, you've got yourself a stalker.

When and if this happens, it's going to be hard to rationalize with her. You can try and have a talk, but be very forward and let her know that the relationship has ended. But understand that, more than likely, she will wig out, cry and act just plain weird.

Best to nip this in the bud to begin with. If you get any weird *Fatal Attraction* vibes, call it an early night and go home.

Another thing about women is that they can get insulted at the smallest things. Maybe you forgot to tell her how nice she looks or whatever then, before you know it, she's throwing a fit. When this happens, apologize and smile, let her rant and rave and then change the topic of conversation. She should get the hint and apologize. This chick is probably not crazy but just a little hotheaded, as most women are. Be prepared for that.

What we learned:
- Some chicks might be stalker material.
- It's best to leave these chicks alone.
- Women can and will get insulted at the smallest things. Learn to deal with it.

Chick flicks.

Yes, you can. Endure them. Be a man. Be strong. And take her to see that damn movie. You can nap through it if you like. If she asks what you think, say, "It was good. What did *you* think?"

See what you're doing here? Yeah, you're getting smarter.

First date. First nervous breakdown.

Before I say anything else, let me say this: going out with a woman for the first time is very similar to going on a job interview. You have to be relaxed but be aware that you're trying to make the best impression. Don't do anything on a first date that you wouldn't on a job interview. Act sociable but never overbearing or too eager.

A cutie I know told me this, "The first date is always the worse. I don't know why, maybe it's because we don't know each other and there is always expectation and tension. But if the guy's cool and nice and he pays for dinner and keeps his hands to himself, then I might consider going on a second date. I hate to admit it, but if he does anything on that first date that I don't like, there *is* no second date after that."

Harsh reality there. But very insightful. The point is, if you like this chick, do everything in your power to get that second date and, hopefully, a third. After the third date, more than likely, you're gonna get to see her boobies.

First of all, bring her a little something that lets her know you appreciate her taking the time to go out with you, but not something corny like a teddy bear.

Things that you can give her:
- A bouquet of flowers—daisies, lilies, etc. but not a rose. (Roses are serious and you want this to be fun. You can send her roses later on.)

- A small box of good chocolates. (Godiva for instance.)
- A CD of oldies music.

The most important thing on a first date is to let her take the lead. Sit back, relax and enjoy the evening. Ask her about herself. She loves to talk, after all. (If you haven't learned anything by now, you should have learned that.) Ask her about her job, her family, her friends, her doll collection, what movies she likes. There is a plethora of information stored inside her head and all you have to do is ask. But don't interrogate her—just allow her the opportunity to talk by carrying on a conversation as you would with anyone else.

It's all about her, her, her. Make it about her and you are on your way. Make it all about you and she won't care. Act like a jerk, don't expect to get laid.

If she's shy and doesn't talk much, maybe suggest a movie. Afterwards, she might come out of her shell. It'll give you something to talk about. Shy girls are tough. You can never tell what's going on inside their noggins. Good luck with those ones.

On your first date, you should make all the arrangements. You should pick her up right on time. (Never early and most certainly never late.) You know she won't be ready and while she's finishing up, look around her place and find out what kind of girl she is. Does she have a roommate? A cat? Why does she have so many pillows on the couch? And what's with all the candles?

Once she appears, she is going to want a compliment from you because she just spent a long time getting ready and she changed five times before settling on this outfit.

Take a few seconds to take her in. She does look mighty fine! Don't hesitate to tell her how nice she looks. Don't just say, "You look good." Say, "Wow, you look great!" But, on the other hand, don't gush! A nice, simple compliment will do and she will appreciate this.

Once in the car, if you're nervous and can't think of anything to say, say, "I just got this CD. Do you like Sinatra?"

Turn it on but keep the speakers low. You don't want to have to yell over the music to be heard. This will take the pressure off and help both of you to relax.

Remember, she's just as nervous as you, if not more so! Be considerate and nice and keep your distance so she'll begin to trust you. Building trust with a lady is a big thing. Do that and you're in.

Now it's time for you to take charge. Tell her what you've got planned for the evening as you're driving to your destination. Smile and ask her about her day. Let her do the talking and act like you're very interested in what she has to say and just not in what she has under that dress.

Of course, you are going to take her to a nice restaurant. Pull up and if it has valet parking, go for it. This will impress her. It impresses me, anyway.

Once inside the restaurant, you know to pull her chair out for her and to let her sit first, right? I knew you did. Good boy. Now, sit down and have a nice meal. And as you're enjoying your meal, start looking for the signs.

There are innumerable ways to tell if she likes you:
- Is she touching your arm? Holding your gaze?
- Is she laughing at your little jokes?
- Is she asking questions about your life?

Women think that all you want is to get laid. Sure, she's right to a certain degree, isn't she? However, you have to show her you *want* to know her first. All that good sex can come later. Show her that you're willing to take the time to get to know her.

Have a good time and when you take her home, give her a peck on her cheek at the door, if she offers it to you. If not, date's over and so is your impending relationship. Always wait until the end of the date to make a move. Don't try to hold her hand. Even this small gesture is a signal to her that you're moving too fast.

She might just ask you inside for a cup of coffee. If so, go for it. But don't think that just because she's asking you in that you're going to get laid. Just think that it's for a cup of coffee. Never assume anything. If she wants you, let her come to you. Don't jump *her* bones. Let her make the first move. Watch for signs. If she's touching your arm and smiling or leaning over in a way so you can catch a glimpse of her luscious breasts, she probably wants it. If not, she just wants to talk some more, you poor thing.

A few important things to never do on dates:

- Don't do drugs. They can make you impotent. They're also illegal.
- Don't drink too much. This will make you stupid and impotent as well.
- Don't just stare at her cleavage all night. Look into her eyes a few times.
- If you spill something, just laugh it off. Don't freak out over it.

Now you've got the first one done. *Phew.* Aren't you glad that's over? What about the next one? Just before you leave, ask her, "Would you like to do this again?" If you've played your cards right, she should reply in the affirmative. If not, she should tell you no. If yes, tell her that you'll call her and thank her for a lovely evening.

On your next date, do something creative. Do something fun and special. And always plan it from start to finish. Just because she's in control, doesn't mean you can't take charge or that you shouldn't. (At least when it comes to making the arrangements.)

Important tip every man should know: Never expect sex or even a kiss on the first date. Even some girls who are absolute freaks won't kiss on the first date. Be a gentleman. Be nice. Keep your hands to yourself and your pants zipped. If she unzips them, then, hey, let her do what she has to do.

What we learned:
- Treat your first date as you would a job interview.
- Be a gentleman the entire time by opening her car door first, pulling out her chair, etc.
- Bring her a small, nice gift that's not too tacky.
- Let her do most of the talking but don't interrogate her.

Your first kiss.

The first kiss is so very important and so very sweet. It's the first time your lips meet hers and the only time you are going to get to prove yourself. Do it right the first time and she will be coming back for more.

But first, you need the signal from her that it's okay. You'll know when it's cool where there's usually a moment of silence and then a connection with the eyes.

After you've gotten the signal, initiate that first kiss. Do it slowly, but like it's the only thing on your mind. Like there is nothing in the world you'd rather be doing. Look at her like there's no one else around (if you're lucky, there won't be) and don't ask if you can do it. Just look her right in the eye, bend down and pull her to you. She will swoon. I don't know what it is about having a guy pull you to him that is so sexy, but just know it is.

Once your mouth is on top of hers, there are two ways to go about it. One is to give her a nice, soft mouth kiss with no tongue. Just pucker up and press your lips against hers softly and then pull back. See if she wants another. If her eyes are still closed, she does. The other is to give her a gut-wrenching, weak in the knees kiss.

And let nature take its course.

Once you're done with that first kiss, pull back and stare her directly in the eyes. If she hasn't asked you in, tell her, "I had a great time tonight. I hope we can do it again." And if you gave her a good kiss, you will.

What we learned:
- No slobbering, tongue kisses.
- Something nice and soft at first.

Safe sex.

If you get lucky, be safe and *always* insist on a condom. You know that a woman can get pregnant, don't you? And you know how that works, right? If not, go ask your mother about it and she'll set you straight.

Also, diseases. You know that you can contract certain disease from sex, right? Yeah, like the clap and all kinds of icky stuff. If you have no clue as to what I'm talking about, go look it up on the internet. There's a whole world of information just waiting for you.

Be informed. Be smart. Be safe.

What to do in the bedroom.

It might be a good thing to know that women are hard-wired for sex just like you. Take a minute to get your head around that. Yes, women want it just as much as men. Believe it or not, women love sex. I can attest to this. I know a woman in her sixties who talks of nothing else. Don't get grossed out, this only validates what I'm saying.

The #1 rule you must accept: Woman are in control. *Flip side:* She wants you to take it—in the bedroom. But don't be too aggressive at first. Never jump the gun—or her bones—until she's given you the greenlight. Just a touch to let her know you're not a sissy. Be subtle. Most women—generalizing here—want a man to dominate them once they're between the sheets. She *wants* you to rock her world. Give her something memorable and she'll come back for more. And if she never wants to see you again, she will definitely keep your number around when she needs some sex.

Before any of this can happen, you need to get yourself prepared to give her an evening of sensual delights. Read sexy erotica. Women usually write erotica, so if you're thinking Henry Miller, don't. Women erotica writers know what turns women on and they put it (sometimes explicitly) in their books. Note: Don't take BDSM literally unless she asks—and she might. Bringing in a pair of handcuffs or some rope will scare the crap out of her. Now if she does it to you, hang on for the ride. There are many, many kinky girls out there. They can't wait to get their hands on you.

So, once you get to the sex, just let nature take its course. But be aware of the body you're groping. You have to understand that there aren't just two parts of a woman—her vagina and her boobs. There are various gateways—places that often don't get touched but bring out the lust—to her sexuality.

A woman's gateways:
- Her neck. (Always use a flat tongue as you kiss/suck at her neck.)
- The small of her back. (Kiss it, lick it, worship it.)
- Her inner thighs. (Umm...just a light finger touch.)
- The back of the knees. (Kiss them lightly.)

Be sure to pay attention to these. If you do, you'll have her swooning. And that means she'll come back for more.

What we learned:
- Be sure to use a condom.
- Read some erotica written by women.
- Take charge of the sex. Be the man in the bedroom.
- Women like sex just as much as men.
- Take care with a woman's gateways.

Beautiful women abroad.

Just something to consider. Another good way to meet some lovely ladies is to travel. Women who reside in other countries will find you more appealing than their native man. It's the English accent principal. Over here, it sounds charming. Over there, it sounds ordinary. You, being a foreigner to her native land, could stand a good chance of hooking up because you're not from around there.

Once you meet a lovely girl, ask her to show you around the city if she has time. Or ask her if she'd like a drink. And let it go from there. The same rules apply.

Once you've got her here's how to keep her.

These next few chapters are going to concentrate on how to keep your new girl once you've found her. Listen carefully and you could very well have the love of your life eating from the palm of your hand. Having a girl you can call your own is like nothing else. No more lonely Saturday nights. No more whining about never getting laid. You're getting laid all the time now because you and she are, as they say, pair bonding. Dare I say it? You and she are...*falling in love.*

Now what? How do you even begin to understand her inner workings? If you thought trying to date was hard, this might be a little tougher. Because now she isn't always acting like she did on the first few dates. And she wants to do this thing called "talking".

Oh, boy. We've got more work to do. Let's step to it.

The bitch is back: Dealing with PMS.

If you've been dating her for a while, there will come a day when your woman acts a little...*off*. She might act crazy, be bitchier than normal and not respond to your lecherous advances. This little hell is fondly known as PMS. There will be times when your woman is going crazy and this is because her hormones have been kicked into overdrive. She's just finished ovulating and that damned egg is about to drop but before it does, she must endure torment and despair for a few days.

Most men don't have a clue as to what PMS is all about. And, let's be honest, you really don't *want* to know anything about it, do you? Well, tough.

Let me tell you what it's like. It's like the whole world is pissing you off and you feel as though you could bite a ten-penny nail in half. Nothing makes sense and everything is annoying. Your breasts are so sore you can't even touch them. And then you get zits and you gain five pounds for no reason. Your belly swells and, on top of that, you can't get enough chocolate or salty foods. It's like you're walking around with a perpetual black cloud hanging over your head and there's nothing you can do about it. So, you cry and cry and then feel stupid about it all. After it's over, you hope no one got hurt. Body count, please?

Sounds fun, doesn't it? You try being a woman for one day and you'll be thankful for us in ways you could never imagine.

The best thing you can do: Give her her space! Back off her for a few days. Tell her to call you when she wants to talk. Expect her to pick fights with you. Her hormones are going insane right now and she is not herself. Anything *can* and *will* set her off, especially if you leave socks lying around.

How to tell if she's PMSing—well, there shouldn't be any doubt but if there is:
- She's snappy.
- Her belly swells.
- She may get a few zits.
- She just told you she hates your guts and all you did was ask her if she wanted a foot rub.

Don't take it personally. She's not herself right now. Forgive her and move on. And no, you can't touch her boobies right now. They are tender and sore as all get out and that's why she's grumpy. You'd be grumpy, too.

This doesn't necessarily mean she is going to try to make your life a living hell, but if you do something to get on her nerves—like heavy breathing—she might. Just stay your distance, ask *once* if anything is wrong and know she'll snap out of it in a few days. Be forgiving of anything bitchy she says during this time. She doesn't mean it, okay? I know it hurts, but she'll make it up to you later.

Now let's touch on the other subject: Her period. Do not put this book down and run away! You should know what this is all about and if you don't, take a class or something. But, more importantly, don't make her feel weird because of it. It's natural. (And you'll probably be happy when it comes every month—that means she's not knocked up!) All women have to have to deal with it each and every month. No wonder we're almost crazy.

Do her a favor and keep a bottle of ibuprofen around for her cramps. And some ice cream. And ask if she would like a foot rub and then give her the best foot rub around. Be gentle and kind with her while all this is going on and if you are, you'll never get rid of this bitch. She's not going to let a good guy like you get away.

Also, ask her if there's anything she wants you to do for her. Like buying her groceries. Or watering her plants. Or helping her around the house. And if she wants you to pick up some tampons, do it. Everyone knows they're not for you.

Chances are, she won't want to have sex once she's on the rag but if she does, just put a towel down. (Women do sometimes get horny during this time of the month.) Women don't bleed quarts and quarts of blood but it can get a little messy. And don't get grossed out about it, either. It's hard enough on us without having you go, "Ick!"

But the most important thing you can do is be understanding of her monthly curse and just try to ignore her screaming at you about the toilet seat. (Which should *always* be left down.)

What we learned:
- PMS is a living hell. Chances are, when she has it, your life will be a living hell as well.
- Don't make her feel bad about her period.
- Be nice and considerate during these times.
- Stay out of her way.
- If she bites your head off, know it's the hormones talking. She'll be back to herself in a few days.

Mystery date.

After you've been seeing your girl for a while, you might want to spice things up. (A little while is a few months, not a few weeks.) One good way to make her squeal like a little girl is to schedule a Mystery Date.

All women go ga-ga over this stuff. It's like, "He cares so much, he told me we were going to have a Mystery Date." What's in it for you? Just a night of hot, intense sex is all. You game?

You will schedule the Mystery Date but, of course, you won't tell her anything about it. Just ask her out for the night and tell her you are going on a Mystery Date. If she asks what you're talking about, just say, "It's a mystery, baby. If I told you, it wouldn't be a mystery, would it?"

Okay, here's how to do it. First of all, figure out how much cash you have to spend. Next, see what your city has to offer. If there's nothing much you can schedule, like a tour of the aquarium after hours, maybe buy a couple of tickets to Vegas and get a nice suite with champagne on ice when you arrive. If you can do a limo, then you are going to be the man!

If Vegas is out of the question and you don't have much cash, look around at your other options. Does your city have a riverboat? You can do any attractions that neither of you have been to since you were little kids. Or take her to a theme park. Anything that would surprise her and isn't the standard "dinner and a movie." You could also get a fancy hotel suite with a Jacuzzi. Just be sure to go get the key before you take her there.

Mystery Dates are good for anniversaries or if you feel her attention is waning a little. They're also good anytime, but especially at the first of a relationship. Do stuff like this and you'll never get rid of her. You have been warned.

What we learned:

- Organize a mystery date and you will have the happiest girl in the world.

Seduction 101.

Obviously, this isn't first date kind of stuff. Once you've been seeing a girl for a while—and have already gotten the preliminary sex over—give her a special night. Women love romance even though most guys just don't get it. We've been fed this stuff from movies and TV since we were little girls and it's not going to change anytime soon. We want our man to cater to us occasionally and if he does, we'll certainly cater to him, in more ways than one. So, how to do it? That's why I'm here.

Seduction is a big word. Oh, boy, it reeks of soft porn and soft lighting. It also spells *l-u-s-t.* And no one these days can get enough of that. What can you do to seduce your girl? Why not set a date up at your house and romance her? And why should you do it? Because women love to be pampered as much as men love to have sex. Pamper her and get a wild and crazy night of hot sex. You game?

Elements needed for seduction:
- Candlelight.
- Soft smiles.
- A clean-shaven face. (As well as a clean body and a clean pad.)
- Some good food.
- A nice bottle of wine. Maybe even a good bottle of champagne to have after dinner.
- Nice music playing in the background. And by nice, I don't mean Kenny G.

- A willing partner.
- Some soft cushions on the floor.
- A bottle of scented oils with which to rub her.
- A classic movie like *Breakfast at Tiffany's*.

First off, cook a nice meal. It doesn't have to be anything with a special crème sauce; it can be a couple of choice steaks. (If she's vegetarian, cook something she can eat.) If you can't cook, order from a caterer and have a lavish table set for her with a nice set of silverware and dishes. If you don't have a nice set of any of this...you know what you have to do.

You're doing all this not only to get her into bed but to make her feel special. Make her feel like somebody special and you'll feel like somebody special by the end of the night.

When she arrives, greet her at the door with a good glass of wine, kiss her cheek and take her jacket. If she asks if she can help with anything say, "Oh, no, I've got it taken care of. You sit and relax."

I am telling you, saying something like this to a woman is the smartest thing a man can do. And it's also a good idea to tell her how good she looks. It's important to know that one reason women just don't jump in the sack with everyone is that they feel insecure about their bodies. Telling her how lovely she looks will help her build confidence about her body.

Once dinner is ready, sit down and serve her. That's right. Make a fuss over her, like you want everything to be just right. But if you drop a spoon or burn the steaks, laugh it off. This is supposed to be fun for *both* of you. (And if you do burn the steaks, order a pizza. You can still serve it on your nice plates and eat by candlelight.)

During dinner, as always, encourage her to talk about herself. How was her day? How was work? How was this and how was that? Smile often like you enjoy listening and add to the conversation about your day as well. Don't bring up the fact that your boss chewed you out over something, either. You can cry about that later. Keep it light and easy.

Now for dessert. Something really, really good and something really, really chocolate. You might want to buy it because making deserts is an art most of us don't practice. Give her the first slice and pick up her fork and ask if you can feed her the first bite. She should say yes. Feed her, hand her the fork and then eat yours.

We all know that the best part of the relationship is the beginning, when neither one of you can get enough of each other. Mmmm...*yum!* Just look at her like she is the only woman on earth. Wow. Makes any girl weak on the knees. Pay attention to her, to her needs. Ask if she would like more wine and pour her more wine. Little things add up. Paying attention to the details will make her know you are one special guy.

By now, both of you should be feeling it. Proceed into the living room where you have set the mood with candles. Why not buy a few nice, chenille throws and a few lush pillows for the floor? I think you should. Lead her over and sit down to watch a movie. Bring the bottle of wine and hit play.

After you're both settled in, glance over at her and ask if she'd like a massage. She is not going to turn you down. Ask her if she'd like you to use the scented oils. If yes, ask her to raise her shirt up and lie down on top of the pillows. Position yourself and give her a good rub. Take your time doing this. She'll want you there all night, believe me. No good woman turns down a free massage.

And then let nature take its course. If she doesn't want a massage, pop the movie in, sit back and relax. And let her come to *you.*

What we learned:

- Seduce a woman with wine, backrubs and good food.
- Make her feel special.
- In turn, she will make *you* feel special.

Keep your eyes to yourself.

One of the main things that piss women off is when men look at other women. I know men look at other women all the time. I know it's your natural instinct. However, most women don't know this and think the reason you're looking at the other chick is because:

- She's prettier.
- Has bigger breasts.
- You like her better.
- You really don't want to be with her.
- You think that she's a big, fat ugly cow.

If this happens and she catches you, don't try to reason with her and don't tell her, "I wasn't looking at her!" She knows you were. Maybe explain it's just natural for men to do that (because it is) but don't expect her to buy it.

Or, maybe, just apologize and explain how much you care for her.

When you've been in a relationship for a while, stuff like this doesn't matter as much. For now, she is the only woman in the world. Treat her as such if you want to get some.

Another thing: Just because you're going out regularly doesn't give you a full license to start treating her badly. Never pick doing something with your buddies over doing something with her, especially in first part of relationship. Women keep score like nobody's business.

What we learned:

- Try not to be too obvious when looking at other women.
- If she catches you, shrug it off.
- Women can and will get very jealous over this sort of behavior.
- Don't start treating her badly just because you've been going out for a while.

Buy her gifts.

Women have a strange relationship with gifts. Most women want to know how you feel and how much you care. If you say it, it's good, but if you accentuate it with a small gift here and there, it's better.

Materialistic? Not at all.

When we were living off the land way back in those cave man days, men would bring women things—meat, furs, firewood—and the women would have sex with these thoughtful men. Prostitution? Hardly. A way to live is more likely.

Today women don't need you to bring them meat or firewood. But they want to make sure you know how good you got it and one way to tell them is to buy them stuff. Don't like the sound of this? Live your life alone.

You don't have to spend much. Just a little something. A good box of chocolates, a bouquet of roses, good stuff like that.

This should be pointed out: Do *not* overindulge her. Just a little gift here and there, not something every single day or every week. Maybe once a month buy her something like a photography book or an artist's kit if she mentions wanting to paint. The point is to listen to what she's saying. She's dropping hints all the time about stuff she wants. And know that all women love Gucci or any other of those high priced handbags. If you can afford a nice Gucci wallet or a purse or even a keychain at some point, you are going definitely going to get on her good side. (Only buy Gucci on the big days—Christmas, Valentine's or for her birthday. Also, keep the receipt in case she wants to trade it for another bag.)

Think your gifts through and if you can't come up with something good for her birthday—*which is the most important holiday of the year*—go buy her a gift certificate at the mall where she can spend it in any shop she likes. Make it for a good amount, too, at least a hundred bucks. Ten bucks ain't gonna cut it. Now for a very important message: When you present the gift certificate, buy her a funny or sweet card to go along with it. And when you present it, buy her a bouquet of flowers and a small box of chocolates. Put all of this into a nice gift bag and you will have a happy girl on your hands.

Or...

Tell her you would like to buy her some lingerie but don't know her size. Then go with her to the lingerie store and have her try on a few things. (It gets sexy in those dressing rooms, just let me tell you.) Let her pick out what she likes and then pay for it. After all, it's for you, too, isn't it? Well, it's mostly for you.

You can attempt to buy lingerie on your own but unless you're a smart man and steal one of her bras and a pair of panties to help you out once you hit the store, you'll probably end up getting the wrong size. (And don't ever steal a pair of her panties for other reasons, okay?)

Valentine's Day is a huge deal to women. You can buy her a gift but always, always include a card, some roses (a dozen is always good if you can afford it) and some form of chocolate. Also, a good meal is in order.

After you've been together a little while, know that it's time to spend a little extra. She wants jewelry and not some crap you got out of a bubble gum machine. Sure, at first this may be cute but if you give her something cheap and ugly for her birthday, expect to catch hell.

Diamonds. You can get a nice little ¼ carat pair of earrings for not that much in most jewelry shops at the malls around the holidays (especially Mother's Day). This is a nice, little gift but be warned, buying diamonds of any kind spells commitment. It might scare her off. Or it might make you think twice. If you don't want to buy diamonds, think gemstones—sapphires, rubies, etc.

Just think your gifts through and if you can't come up with anything, use a gift certificate. And you know to never, ever buy her a frying pan, right? If you do, expect it to be slammed against your head.

One last thing, make sure that the gifts are presented on the right days. If you give it to her early, you better make sure that you have something else for her on the actual holiday. And never give her anything late.

What we learned:
- Women have a weird relationship with gifts.
- Buy her gifts but never overindulge her.
- Buy diamonds only after you've been seeing her for a while.
- If you can't think of anything, buy her a gift certificate to the mall.

Juggling two girls at once.

Good grief. This sounds like the plot for a romantic comedy gone awry. You are in some hot water now. For some reason, you've got two hotties interested in you at the exact same time. You can't decided which one you prefer, in fact, you like *both* of these chicks. I can hear you now: *Can I have both of them? Please? I promise to be real good!*

No, you can't. Who do you think you are? A rock star? Just because you feel like one doesn't mean you can act like one.

All I can tell you is that it will eventually blow up in you face. You can try the juggling act and it might work for a little while, but be a man and make a choice, otherwise, your women will make the choice for you and you might just find yourself alone.

What we learned:
- If you try to juggle two girls at once, you've just asking for it.

If you screw up...

Being a man, women do expect this of you. Something will happen and you'll forget some anniversary or you'll say something she perceives as rude and then she'll be obligated to tear you a new one. Or, you might just get the silent treatment.

Whatever you do, if she's in love (or like) with you, she will forgive you—e*ventually.* But *y*ou will have to work for it, believe me. It will blow over after she's made you "pay" for it for a while. Women do this so you know she won't take any crap. It's a protective measure and a test. Women love giving men tests. I think just to see how badly they will fail. And then they grade you, rarely on a curve.

Another thing. If you hurt your woman, you will live to rue the day. Hurt her and she'll turn into the evil bitch queen from hell. Women really get their feathers up when it comes to this stuff.

Whatever you did, whether it was cheating or being rude, get down on your hands and knees and ask forgiveness. Women are sensitive. Get used to this idea. But, hey, you can't live without them.

What we learned:
- When you screw up, admit to it and ask for forgiveness.
- Eventually, she'll forget about it. Maybe.

Everybody's somebody's fool.

It's true. The time might come when you find out that your honey wants to break it off. In fact, she played you. She made a fool out of you. You once worshipped her and now you hate her guts. She dumped you after all you did for her. She gave you up even after you put up with her PMS!

I'm sorry, baby, but it happens.

Don't go crazy. Have your feelings and then let them go and find yourself another woman. But always, always do this: Be the bigger person. Continue to be a gentleman. Don't let her know how she got to you. Revenge is a dish best served cold and when she sees you out with your new girl, she is going to be green with envy.

What if she cheated on you? Well, you know, it happens and it could happen to you. Cheating is a very sensitive subject, especially when you are in the beginning stages of a relationship because that's when you're pair bonding. So, to have her go out and do some other guy is really going to hurt.

My advice to you is to think long and hard. Don't go crazy with jealousy. It's going to be hard not to go a little bonkers, but try to keep yourself calm. She's human and she made a mistake, okay? If she leaves you for some other guy, then good riddance. She's probably going to cheat on him as well.

Maybe she just had a weak moment or got really drunk and the guy took advantage of her, so listen to what she has to say. I know you will be insane at this time and you're not going to be very reasonable. If you can find it in your heart to forgive her, forgive her. If you can get through this, your relationship will be stronger because of it.

If you can't get through it without calling her all kinds of hurtful names, then let her go. Don't ask her to stick around so you can emotionally abuse her. Why have all these big fights if you're going to end up breaking up anyway? Why risk hurting yourself—and her—more?

But know, we are all human and all of us make mistakes. If you really like this girl, you will find it in your heart to forgive her. And if you can be man enough to shrug it off as a mistake, then you're the kind of man every woman wants.

This is *not* to say that you should be a doormat. If she's a serial cheater and does it more than once, it might be best to cut her loose. As I have said, women do like sex as much as men and there are women out there who sleep around as much as men. I believe it's just in some people to cheat. Maybe your girl is one of the cheaters. Maybe she just can't help herself. But because she does this, don't do the old double standard thing and call her a whore or a slut. Men get away with this all the time and, just because she does it, doesn't necessarily mean she's a bad person. She just likes sex. A lot. Maybe you could try one of those open relationship things. And if that's not your bag, move on.

And a word about jealousy. You will find yourself getting jealous over her. That's okay but if you take it too far—by threatening her or accusing her of sleeping around—you really need to see a psychologist. Love will inspire a little jealousy, but nothing over the top. It should come and if it does, feel it and let it go. Never let it get the best of you. If you start accusing her of things, she's going to walk out the door and never come back. You don't want that, do you? Only a truly insecure person will have a fit if he thinks his girl is checking out another guy. A real man smiles because knows she's going home with him. And if you always treat her right, you will have no reason to worry at all.

So, if something happens and you break up, take it as a life experience and move on. Be a man and let her go. If she comes back…you know the rest. Don't haggle her, don't cry and whine. Don't stalk her! If she leaves you after all you've done, she is a bitch who doesn't know how good she had it. Once she realizes it, she might beg you to come back. And that will be your decision.

It's going to hurt for a while but think of all you've learned being with her. Apply all the good stuff to your next relationship and let some other woman reap the benefits.

What we learned:
- Some relationships weren't meant to be.
- If it's not working out, move on and find another woman.
- If she cheats on you, ask yourself if you can forgive her and if not, don't put her through any kind of hell over it. Sometimes cheating is just about getting off and not about finding a new partner.
- Be careful with jealousy. If you find yourself in a mad rage, get away from your woman and cool off. Fights can sometimes escalate to the point of violence. *Never hit her.*

Breaking up.

I knew this was going to happen.

You found her, you dated her, you got laid. Now she's not jiving with you and your world and you want to dump her. Maybe you've got another girl you like better. Whatever the reason, who cares? You don't want to be in a relationship with this girl anymore and continuing on with it is pointless and destructive. And, if you don't like her but keep on dating her, that's like, a bad thing to do. It's like you're lying to her.

Be a man and break it off before it goes any further.

As with asking a chick out, there is no easy way to break up. For all you know, she wants to break up with you. But don't be a jerk and wait around for her to start hating your guts. Don't be a jerk and stop returning her calls or avoiding her. Make a clean break. Give her a call, tell her you don't want to see her anymore and expect a major butt chewing. Take it like a man and allow her to yell and scream for a good five minutes. Let her call you a slime ball and then be on your way. Tell her it was nice knowing her and you hope there is no hard feelings and then hang up and move on with your life. Believe me, this is the easiest way to go about it. Don't ever play mind games or any of that. Do it like a man.

Next!

What we learned:

- If it's time to move on, let her know upfront. Don't play any stupid games like not retuning calls. Just tell her, "It's been nice but I need to move on. I'm breaking up with you."
- Be prepared for a big fight when you break up.
- Let her have her say and take it like a man, then excuse yourself and get on with your life.
- Always be a gentleman and she'll get over it.

The three scariest words.

I love you. I love *you*. I *love* you. I LOVE YOU! Hey, I love you, too.

What fear that those three little words incite in men. It's like the scariest thing in the world. But you need to know that women want to hear this like nothing else. Knowing that you love her is better than a diamond ring. It really, really is. Nothing material can compare to the love-word. Nothing.

But how do you do it? Well, first you have to feel it and if you feel it, you will know it.

Here's what one of my guys did. It was Valentine's Day. He got me a card with a rose on the cover that said, "P.S." Inside, was, "I love you."

That's how he did it. I was, like, shocked. But it was the sweetest thing he could do. Then he would slip it in here and there until I said it back. And that was about it.

Just be cautious and don't do it too soon. This will scare her off. Let it come naturally. When you feel it, say it and don't be afraid to say it. If she says it first, then you're off the hook. However, if she says it first, make sure to say it back *if* you feel it. And you don't feel it, man, you are in for the fight of your life and I can't help you, in fact, no one can. All I can do is tell you to duck for cover.

What we learned:

- Saying "I love you" shouldn't be that big of a deal.
- When you feel it, say it. That way, if she doesn't feel it, you will know whether or not to continue the relationship.
- If you don't feel it, then let her know. That way, she'll know whether or not to continue the relationship.
- If you want to say it, say it, but never too soon.
- I think a good rule of thumb is by the second or third month of dating someone. If you're not feeling it by then, you might not ever.

Your worst nightmare... *Can we talk?*

I, as a woman, have a really hard time understanding why you boys don't like to talk. Sometimes when we say this, we're not looking to bust your balls. Granted, most of the time, we are, but occasionally we are looking for something else and that something could be anything from reassurance—"Of course you're the most beautiful girl in the world!"—to comfort—"Hold me, my tummy hurts."

They want you to listen. Women love to talk more than men. It's biologically true; she uses a lot more words in a day than you do. She is a blabber-mouth. Let me tell you what to do: Take care of her and she will take care of you.

Keep in mind that the day may come when *you* want to talk and, if so, she might not be in the mood.

So, therefore, when your girl asks you to talk, you have not been cornered. Well, sometimes you have been, but let's just say she just wants to get something off her chest. Like are you going to make a commitment to her? I mean, she doesn't want to spend all this time with you if there's not a chance in you marrying her. It's true. It's time. It's that time and boy, you really need to make a decision fast.

So, my advice to you is to make your decision and tell her about it. If you don't want to marry her, be honest so she can dump you and find someone else before her eggs dry up. If you do want to commit but want to wait a while for marriage, tell her that. But if you make a promise, you better hold up on your end of the bargain. And don't drag it out, either. Be a man.

Another thing women do is ask loaded questions. This might be one reason men are scared when it comes to "talking". Say for instance, she asks one day, "Honey, do you think my butt looks fat?" You respond that no, it isn't, in fact, it's perfect. Then the next thing you know, she's screaming at the top of her lungs at you. This is a loaded question. And she's asking it because, more than likely, she wants to start a fight. And there's a reason she wants to fight. It might be because you were rude to her mother on the phone. It might be because she caught you staring at another chick. Whatever it is, it will eventually come out. But not for a while.

Oh, boy. I feel for you when this happens.

Okay, fellas, women do ask loaded questions and there is no way to tell when one is loaded and when one isn't. And the only way you know it was a loaded question is if you get into a fight after a seemingly innocent remark.

When this happens, just sit there and let her go off. Don't block her out—listen to what she's saying because it's very important for her. Don't taunt her and don't start screaming back. Occasionally, take up for yourself and after she's calmed down, tell her, "I didn't say you have a fat butt. What's this really all about? Please tell me. I want to know."

One thing that you need to know is this: When she's going off for no reason, she might be PMSing. But if you ask her, "Is it that time of the month?" understand this will infuriate her even more. Sure, it might be that time of the month, but saying this is a one-way ticket to hell. She knows she's being irrational but she can't help herself. She doesn't want you to not take her seriously because of PMS.

So, let her yell and if she doesn't shut up within fifteen minutes, tell her, "I'm going to take a drive and let you cool off. When I get back, maybe you'll be a bit calmer and then we can talk about it." You're not walking away from her, you're just letting her cool off.

When you get back, if she's stilling wigging out, you might have a problem. Something really must be bothering her. Do your best to get it out of her and let her talk about it. If this doesn't work, I wouldn't recommend standing there and taking her crap for very long. Nobody deserves to be treated like this. Take a stand and tell her you're not going to put up with this. Women will try to push you around. They will try to push your buttons and they will try to hurt you by calling you lame names. If you don't stand up to her right then and there, you're facing a lifetime of being whipped.

Most times when women do this, they simply want to know that you'll stand up for yourself. If you don't respect yourself enough to do it, then why should she respect you? Stand up to her and let her know this isn't cool with you. Never disrespect her or, God forbid, hit her. Just let her know that she's just driving you crazy and you're not going to take it. Be firm about it, too.

What we learned:
- When she wants to talk, let her talk.
- She will ask loaded questions and pick fights.
- Try not to engage her during these times and never ask if it's that time of the month.
- If she doesn't calm down within fifteen minutes or so, tell her you're going to give her a little breathing room and when you get back, you want to talk this whole thing out.
- Talk it out and then get the problem fixed.
- Sometimes, when women pick fights, they want to know that you'll stand up for yourself. Stand up for yourself and be firm. But never harm her when you're doing it. Always maintain respect.

Will you marry me?

No, but *she* might.

So you've found The One. You want to make sure she doesn't get away so the obvious thing to do is ask her if she'd like to get hitched. How do you do it? Well, for starters, you say, "Will you marry me?"

If you want to do it in a special way, my suggestion is that you do it in private. That way, you don't put her on the spot in front of a huge crowd. And, you never know, she could say no and how embarrassing would that be?

Think back to your first date. What did you do? How about you repeat the date, from start to finish? Don't tell her that you're repeating the date and if she catches on with a, "Hey, this seems familiar," just smile and say, "Yeah, it's almost like déjà vu."

But don't say a word.

As the date is coming to a close, take her back to your place which you have stocked with flowers and candles. Once you're there, she'll know what's going on.

So, all you have to do is get down on one knee and ask her, "Would you like to get married? To me, I mean."

You don't have to do it this way, of course, but I think it's romantic. If you choose to do something clever, take a suggestion here and never, ever put an engagement ring in any kind of food. She could swallow or choke on it.

So what happens after you've popped the question and set a date? Don't worry. She will plan it all and all you have to do is show up. In fact, it's probably been planned for years.

Just a note: Before you ask anyone to marry you, it's a good idea to find out how much debt she's in. If she has a nice wardrobe, chances are, she's in debt. You need to find this stuff out because once you're hitched, you're in debt, too. Not that you shouldn't marry her if she's in over her head, but I think it's good to always be upfront and honest about all matters, including financial.

What if you're not getting married but want to move in together? Be prepared to change, boy. She doesn't want to pick up after you or cook every night. And all that stuff I told you to get rid of at the beginning of the book? It's time to do it.

Moving in together shouldn't be that big of a deal. In fact, it should save both of you money on your rent. The important thing to remember is to never take her for granted just because you've closed the deal by taking this step. Always take her out for dinner and continue to pay for it. Always buy her flowers and make a big deal out of her birthday. Treat her with respect and, occasionally, bring her breakfast in bed. Make your time together special. Most importantly, be a good man to her and, in turn, she will be a good woman to you. What else could you ever want?

What we learned:

- When you ask her to marry you, do it in a special way that's memorable so she can look back and smile.
- It might be a good idea to see how badly your girl is in debt.
- If you want to move in with her, just ask her. This one shouldn't be a big deal at all and

combining your resources can help the both of you save for a house or a nice vacation.

- After you've sealed the deal, continue to treat her like she's your girlfriend by taking her out for dinner and buying her gifts occasionally. Just because you put a ring on her finger does not make her your maid.

- By doing this, you'll save yourself bundles of fights because if you're not taking her for granted, there's not much she can bitch at. (Unless she's PMSing.)

The engagement ring.

You did it. You asked her to marry her. Or you're planning on it. Or whatever. It's time to buy that ring that is going to set you back a pretty penny.

The ring might not seem like a big deal to you, but to women it is very important. They want one to show off and they want the best. If they don't get one, they feel like they've been cheated out of it.

Even if you can't afford a big one, you do need to get her something. Maybe tell her this is a promise ring until you can afford a better one. Let her know that you want her to know that you love her and want her to have the best, when you can better afford it.

This should be good enough and if it's not, she's a little too materialistic. Women know that not all men can afford a five carat ring. Most women don't mind as long as they have the promise you'll do better when you can. If she's in love with you, that is.

But which one? White gold? Gold? Platinum? Listen to this. Unless you have immaculate taste, ask her friend or mother or sister to help you out.

You should expect to pay a lot of money for that itty-bitty thing but rest assured, if you don't buy her one, she will give you hell about it for the rest of your life. And if you can't afford one, why are you getting married?

What we learned:
- If you do ask her to marry you and don't know what kind of ring to buy, go to her friend, mother or sister.

Is all this worth it? I mean, really?

Do you even have to ask? I mean, *come on.* Of course it's worth it! What are you? Some heartless jerk? I know what you're thinking, *What am I getting out of all this? It seems like a lot to go through just to get laid every once in a while.*

You just don't get it, do you?

Believe me, once you fall in love and/or become a dating machine, you will know the answer to that. However, there are some other perks involved as well.

So, what *do* you get out of all of this? She will become your number one ally, your number one fan. She will probably never worship you—at least not until there are no more cute boy bands out there—but she will bring your life joy and passion and all that other good grown-up stuff you've been missing.

She will not, however, fix your life. She can't make you into a better man. That's *your* job. But she can help you to be a better man.

Once you've found your honey, your days will be like New Year's Eve. You'll want to celebrate for no reason. You'll want to kick up your heels and act the fool. You'll be telling everyone Merry Christmas even in the summer. You'll feel like skipping like a little girl. Falling in love is just like make believe. It's the best damn feeling in the world and a feeling no one can get enough of.

Well, at least until the infatuation wears off. And that's another story. When you start having sex, you will never experience anything as nice as it is in the beginning. And most times, you won't even have to beg for it. There is nothing like falling in love and nothing like having the woman of your dreams love your back. It will blow your mind.

She's yours to have and to hold. She's yours. Get used to it.

But, you're saying, *but...it's still a lot of work.*

If she falls in love and marries you, she will be picking up after you for the rest of her life. Think about *that* before you start bitching about how much work this is. It isn't that much work to get the best thing in the world and call it your own.

Just know that when you get it, you'll always be warm in the winter. You'll have someone to ask you how your day was and give a damn if it went bad. You'll have someone to procreate with if you choose!

So, stop your bitching and get off that couch now, boy, and change your life. I don't care if you still think that there is no one out there for you. There *is* someone out there who wants you as much as you want them. Believe that and you're going to make the best boyfriend/husband around. Go on, now.

What we learned:

- Nothing concerning dating or being with a woman is a waste of time.
- You can always learn a thing or two from each of the lassies you date.
- Falling in love with a woman, from what I've heard, makes you feel warm and fuzzy inside.